All you need to know about

CD-ROM

All you need to know about

CD-ROM

by Damien Noonan

Future Publishing Limited
Beauford Court
30 Monmouth Street
Bath
Avon BA1 2BW

All you need to know about CD-ROM

Future Publishing Limited, Beauford Court, 30 Monmouth Street, Bath, Avon BA1 2BW

ISBN 1-85870-059-0

British Library Cataloguing in Publication Data
A CIP catalogue record for this book is available from the British Library

Books Editor Ian Jones

Subbing and layout Rod Lawton & Garrick Webster

Cover design Lisa Nicholls

Printed and bound in the UK by Ashford Colour Press

Contents

How to use this book

It's more than just buying another piece of hardware! Your CD-ROM will completely revolutionise the way you use your PC – and *All you need to know about CD-ROM* will show you all you need to know to explore this new multimedia world.

If you're just starting out you'll discover what to look for in a CD-ROM drive, how to set it up, how it works in theory and how to get it working in practice!. Or if you're upgrading an existing system, this book will build on what you already know to include this latest technology.

All you need to know about CD-ROM also lists many available CD-ROMs and what you can do with them. Damien Noonan was the launch editor of *CD-ROM* Today magazine. He has long been a CD-ROM enthusiast, writes for many of the UK's leading computing magazines and is an acknowledged CD-ROM expert.

Whatever your question, *All you need to know about CD-ROM* is the book with all the answers!

And to make it even easier to use, we've picked out special notes, tips and pieces of advice in bold type, and signposted them with icons in the margins. This is what they mean.

MAKE A NOTE!

Make a note. Most of the things you read get stored away in your head somewhere or other. When you see this icon, though, make sure you store this particular item somewhere prominent. It's quite important.

TOP TIP

Top Tip. There are lots of ways of saving time, money and effort that you'll never see in print. Except here!

What does it mean? Anything to do with the Internet is packed with jargon. You can't get rid of it, you just have to live with it. But that doesn't mean to say you can't explain it...

Warning! You won't see this icon too often, but when you do, pay attention! Ignoring it could cost you time, money or your sanity. And none of us have much to spare of any of those.

Chapter One
Introduction

- Welcome!
- What is CD-ROM?
- What hardware do I need?
- A brief guide to CD-ROM titles

Appearing on a computer screen near you, stars like Prince, David Bowie, Peter Gabriel, Arnie, Humphrey Bogart, Dennis Hopper all feature in CD-ROM titles, along with an enormous range of other people.

Welcome!

Hello and welcome to a book that we hope will help you enter the amazing world of CD-ROM computing.

Getting a CD-ROM drive means far more than just buying another piece of computer hardware. It's no exaggeration to say that it will completely change the way you use your computer.

A CD-ROM drive is easy to fit and even easier to use, and when you've installed it and you start running your first CD-ROM discs, you'll soon discover for yourself that CD-ROM is a radical new medium that opens up all kinds of amazing possibilities.

Probably the key words are 'practical' and 'fun'. CD-ROM applications can be immensely useful, with a wide range of reference titles that put information at your fingertips and make it easy, and quicker than ever before, to find what you want. But with the superb graphics, sound and video that CD-ROM discs are capable of delivering, CD-ROM applications are also more entertaining than anything you've seen on a computer before.

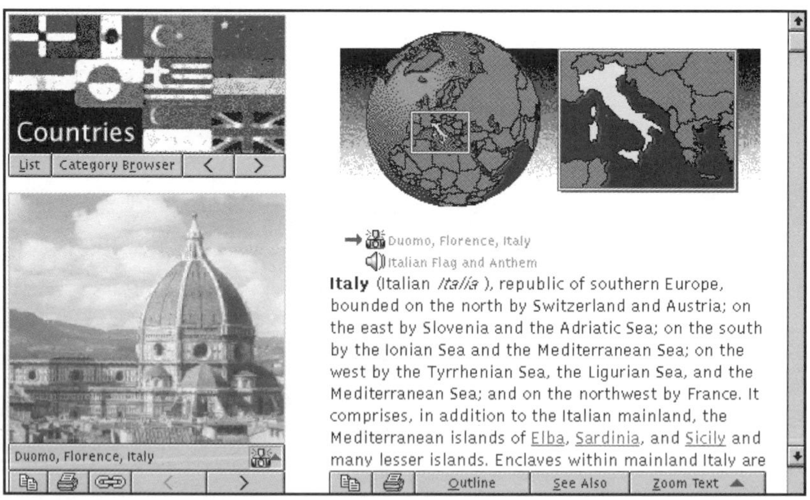

The archechetypal CD-ROM application is the encyclopedia. The immense storage capacity of CD-ROM is used to hold masses of information which you can search through in seconds. Shown here is Microsoft's Encarta '94.

So without further ado, let's take a quick look at the sort of things you can expect to discover in the amazing new world of CD-ROM, and run through some things you'll need to know to start exploring this amazing new world for yourself.

What is CD-ROM?

WHAT DOES IT MEAN?

CD-ROM, which stands for 'Compact Disc Read-Only Memory', means using normal compact discs to store computer data instead of digital audio.

When audio CDs were first introduced, the inventors of digital audio, Philips and Sony, quickly realised that because music CDs stored their music in the form of digital data, the same CDs could easily be used to store computer data instead.

When you put computer data on a CD-ROM disc, you discover that a single CD can store up to 660Mb of data – an astonishing amount of information. This gives CD-ROM the ability to hold massive amounts of text, which makes it ideal for reference works such as encyclopedias and dictionaries. But that space can also be used to store lots of graphics, animation, video, sounds and music, which can be combined to make almost any kind of software far more exciting and enjoyable.

CD-ROM has actually been around since 1985, but it's only since 1993 that it has really taken off, thanks to vast reductions in the price of the hardware, combined with improvements in the technical specification and the availability of a number of truly impressive examples of CD-ROM software which have taken advantage of those technical improvements.

If you're just getting into CD-ROM, you're not alone. It is currently the most vibrant and active area of computing, with more and more people joining in all the time. Apple say that over 70% of people buying a new Macintosh computer now ask for one which has a CD-ROM drive already fitted, while Microsoft are selling tens of thousands of CD-ROM discs and PC owners are buying about 20,000 new CD-ROM drives every month, in the UK alone.

What equipment do I need?

The most popular formats for CD-ROM are PC-compatibles and the Apple Macintosh, though many video games systems are also moving over to using CDs. If you have a PC or Mac already, it should be simple to buy and fit all the extra hardware you need to run the very best CD-ROM software.

If you are a Macintosh owner, so long as you've got a machine that can run a 13-inch 256-colour display and has 4Mb of RAM, you're all ready to go with CD-ROM. All you need to buy is a CD-ROM drive, which will cost about £150, though you might also wish to invest in a pair of amplified stereo speakers so that you get the best out of the superb sound capabilities of CD-ROM.

Virgin's The 7th Guest was one of a new generation of state-of-the-art computer games developed specifically to take advantage of the power of CD-ROM. Even better games are becoming available every day.

A typical multimedia PC set-up looks something like this, except you'd probably want to add a pair of powered speakers to make the most of your CDs' sound quality. The CD-ROM drive is mounted in a spare 5.25-inch drive bay at the front of the machine, and features a motorised tray that slides out for you to put the disc in, just like a hi-fi CD unit.

If you're a PC owner, you need a 25MHz 386 machine or better with 4Mb of RAM, a hard disk drive and an S-VGA accelerated video card. On top of this you will have to add a 16-bit sound card and a CD-ROM drive, preferably with a pair of amplified stereo speakers so that you can hear that glorious CD sound properly. All the extra equipment you need can be yours for less than £300, and if you already have a good gamesplaying PC with sound card installed, you may well only need to buy the CD-ROM drive itself, which will only cost about £150.

What can CD-ROM do?

Just to give you an idea, here's a run-through of some of the different kinds of CD-ROM applications you can expect to come across. We'll start with a few of the 'bonus' features that a CD-ROM drive makes possible, before you even start on the real stuff of CD-ROM itself.

- **You can play normal audio CDs**
- **You can play 'mixed mode' CDs combining computer data and CD hi-fi audio**
- **You can access Kodak Photo CD**
- **You have the option to expand your system to play Video CDs**

The mechanical workings of a CD-ROM drive are identical to a normal CD player, and so with your CD-ROM drive you will be able to play audio CDs too. All CD-ROM drives come with software to run on your computer that plays audio CDs, and you can leave it running in the background when using normal hard disk-based programs, for music while you work!

As well as one or the other, CDs can also store a mixture of computer data and pure CD-DA hi-fi quality audio. This 'mixed mode' system can be used for all sorts of things: games with superb stereo soundtracks; children's songbooks that combine interactive graphics with a compilation of popular children's favourite tunes; and even classical music discs that provide a running commentary on the music.

All modern CD-ROM drives can also play discs that are created by Kodak's new Photo CD system. The way this works is you pop down to Boots or your local Kodak shop, and they can put up to 100 photographs onto a unique, personal CD in digital form. You can then watch a slideshow of your pictures, or use the photographs in graphics and DTP packages to create highly personal designs.

With the addition of an extra piece of hardware costing about £200, your CD-ROM system will be capable of playing the new Video CD digital video discs. This not only means you can watch *Wayne's World* or Pink Floyd in concert on your computer, but also means you have access to special new versions of CD-ROM programs such as encyclopedias that use full-screen, top-quality video as illustration.

Typical CD-ROM applications

- Encyclopedias, reference, 'infotainment'
- State-of-the-art games
- Interactive children's books
- Education and 'edutainment'
- Music and leisure
- Collections of shareware, graphics, photos, videos or sounds
- 'Try before you buy' discs

Encyclopaedias on CD-ROM are now said to be outselling the old-fashioned printed kind by a wide margin, and it's easy to see why. Not only can you search through the entire encyclopedia in seconds to find what you want, but also when you get to the article you're looking for you might discover that it's illustrated with photos, diagrams,

The charming Tuneland is a disc for kids that uses a 'mixed-mode' format, combining CD-ROM computer data and CD-DA hi-fi audio. It features new versions of favourite children's songs performed by top-name musicians, which can also be played on a normal hi-fi CD player.

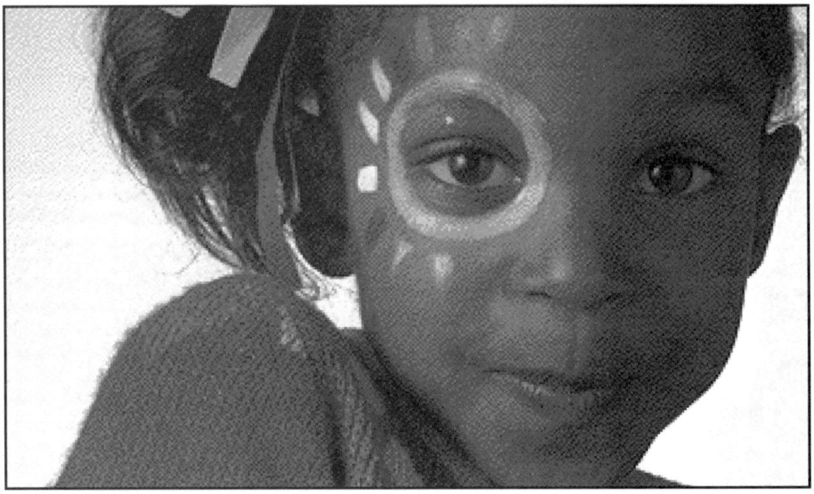

Kodak's Photo CD means you can get your own photographs digitised and stored on a CD-ROM disc so that you can load them into a graphics or DTP program and create something really individual.

animated diagrams, video clips of an event, extracts from the sound archives or clips of music. It makes reference a lot more fun!

There's a wide variety of other reference works available on CD-ROM besides encyclopedias, such as the impressive Oxford English Dictionary, which packs the definitive 21-volume set onto a single disc costing £500!

WHAT DOES IT MEAN?

Besides practical reference, though, there are all sorts of other interesting titles that are the equivalent of non-fiction books, and recognising the fact that we buy this kind of thing for enjoyment as much as practical reference, this kind of disc is often referred to by the strange compound word 'infotainment'.

Whatever your hobby there's likely to be something for you, from the amazing film guide *Cinemania* to topics like ancient history, comic books, dinosaurs, astronomy or space exploration.

One of the most thriving areas of CD-ROM, on the PC especially, is games, which can make outstanding use of the enormous capacity of CD-ROM to create astounding games that are currently the state of the art in computer entertainment. Games like *The 7th Guest* and *Myst* have been responsible for many a user rushing out to buy a CD-ROM drive, and you can also get high-value compilations and collections of games on CD-ROM.

One of the most charming and successful uses of the 'multimedia' idea is the interactive children's book, where animation, narration, sound effects and music all combine to tell the story, but the child can also explore the screen by clicking around with the mouse to set of all sorts of delightful and unpredictable events. Discs such as the Living Books series from Broderbund have charmed many a parent into buying a CD-ROM system for younger children to use – or that's what the parents' claim, anyway!

If storybooks like that are the equivalent of pre-school education, there is also a whole range of educational software for all ages and levels of ability. There are many fun titles for younger children that cover ever-popular subjects like dinosaurs, space rockets and creepy-crawlies, but there are also many genuinely educational discs aimed at use in schools, on topics such as science, history and languages: and these range right up to degree-level reference resources and adult language courses, too.

Entertainment for grown-ups is available in good measure too, and especially music. Not only is there a wide choice of classical music discs, but also many of the biggest names in rock music have started exploring the possibilities of CD-ROM, with Peter Gabriel, David Bowie and Prince all releasing interactive albums in 1994.

Last but not least for this brief run-through, anything a normal computer medium can store, CD-ROM can store better. There are great resources available on CD-ROM to enhance whatever you use your computer for, from massive collections of clip-art and photographs for you to use in graphics and DTP, to huge compilations of shareware programs.

Another fine example of the kind of CD-ROM game that is proving a persuasive reason to buy a CD-ROM drive is Myst, an intellectual adventure into a virtual world where you must solve problems to explore further.

You can also get 'try before you buy' discs with demo versions of all the latest software: if you find something you like, a phone call and a credit card payment will unlock the full version for you, so that you can download it from CD to your hard disk and start using it straight away, with manuals following by post.

Happy hunting!

We've only been able to skim the surface of CD-ROM applications here. One of the pleasures that awaits you is looking through the magazines and catalogues to find the CD-ROM titles that most appeal to you. Elsewhere in this book, you'll find introductions to all the different kinds of software available on CD-ROM, but new discs are released at such a rate that we can't comprehensively list all the different discs of any particular type that are available: the book would be out of date a few days after it was published!

This is where magazines like *PC Plus*, *PC Format*, *PC Answers*, *MacFormat* and *CD-ROM Today* come in. In these magazines you'll be able to read news and reviews of new discs, browse the advertisements for titles that are already on sale, and even try out

If classical music is your thing, you might be interested in a whole range of classical music discs, like Microsoft's Multimedia Stravinsky. As well as music, discs like this include running text commentary that will help you understand the piece, and lots of background information too.

demos of the latest releases from the magazines' cover CDs. *CD-ROM Today* also features a comprehensive buyer's guide to PC and Mac CD ROM titles, which may help you find what you're looking for.

With your CD-ROM drive you'll probably get a few free titles to get you started, but you'll soon be discovering all sorts of enticing new discs that you'll want to spend your hard-earned money on. Read the magazine reviews to find out if they live up to expectations.

And bear in mind that CD-ROM as we know it today is a relatively new medium. Which means that as more and more software developers gain experience, and more and more publishers start producing CD-ROM titles, the quality and choice will increase all the time. The best is yet to come!

Chapter 2
The Compact Disc

- The history of the compact disc
- How CD players and drives work
- Looking after your CDs

Introduction: let's begin at the beginning

We're going to start this chapter with a quick look at the history of the Compact Disc and some details about audio CDs. This section isn't compulsory, so skip it if you wish. But very often it's true that if you understand the background you will find it easier to assimilate the things you really do need to know.

Besides which, there are some pretty interesting tales in the brief but dramatic story of the success of CD. And it's the digital technology behind the familiar, silvery five-inch audio CD that has made CD-ROM possible. And it will continue to make interesting new forms of home entertainment possible, such as the Video CDs which we could soon be using instead of VHS tapes whenever we want to watch a movie – or a music video, or the highlights of the last football season, or whatever else you currently watch on videotape – in the comfort of our own homes.

We'll also explain how CDs work in this chapter, which is of immediate relevance when you're trying to understand CD-ROM; and we'll go on to give you the details of all the different CD-ROM formats and standards, all of which you will find pretty useful when you're buying and using a CD-ROM system.

The compact disc arrives, 1982

The story of CD-ROM really starts with the arrival of the CD – or to give it its full title, Compact Disc Digital Audio – which was seen as a thrilling new leap in hi-fi technology when it was introduced way back in 1982 by electronics giants Philips and Sony.

It's taken quite a while for CDs to really take off, but in 1993 the British Phonographic Industry announced that album sales on CD had reached a new all-time record level in the UK – beating the previous record set in 1978 by vinyl LPs.

Not many people remember that in the late Sixties Philips had developed the compact cassette tape, which they marketed so successfully that it rapidly become a worldwide standard. In fact, however popular audio CDs have become, the most popular format for music sales is still cassette tape, with about 50% of the market. Philips now hoped to make CD audio just as successful as cassettes had become.

However good it is, you still have to sell it...

The experience Philips had gained with the cassette told them that the secret to CD's success would lie in two areas. First, they had to convince the public, through strenuous advertising and public relations efforts, that CD had inherent technical advantages. Second, they had to make CD an 'open technology', which would mean that any electronics manufacturer could build and sell CD players, and any record company could press and distribute CD recordings.

The open technology idea had many direct benefits. For starters, it avoided destructive 'format wars' such as the battle between Sony's Betamax and JVC's VHS video formats. Instead, it harnessed the profit motives of all concerned and put them into a co-operative effort that would help the new medium succeed.

The 'hardware' makers – electronics manufacturers who made CD players – would sell lots of new machines, while the 'software' publishers – the record companies – would be able to cut their costs (with rising oil prices, the production costs of vinyl LPs had risen far faster than these costs could be passed on to a resistant market) as well as charge higher retail prices, and could also re-sell, on the new format, many copies of records that people already owned on outdated vinyl.

It suited everyone concerned, and it also suited Sony and Philips. Even though it was an open technology, they wouldn't be giving it away: a system of licensing fees would ensure the enormous development cost of CD would be recouped, and that CD would make them a profit well into the future. The visible evidence of this arrangement is still apparent on every CD you ever buy: all CDs carry the 'Compact Disc Digital Audio' logo, as they are obliged to by licence arrangements.

The commercial prospects for CD were good, but Philips and Sony still had to convince the public, which they set about doing by playing on the almost mystical witch-doctory of the new technology.

A miraculous new medium?

When it came to acceptance by the public, the CD had a lot on its side straight away, simply because it really did look like a technological marvel. Those shiny silver discs, with their beautiful rainbow diffraction of light, just seemed really space-age. And they were so small, too, compared with the ugly, black twelve-inch vinyl LPs that everyone was used to. Another big plus was that CD players used a laser, which in itself had attractive science-fiction connotations.

And the music was digital… apparently. No-one quite knew what that meant, but it had something to do with computers (and this was round about the time the first real home computers, such as the Sinclair Spectrum and the Amstrad CPC, were taking off) so it must be pretty fancy.

But the main advantages Philips emphasised were the sound quality and the robustness of the new medium.

Most people were all too aware of how fragile vinyl LPs were: how they wore out when you played them, jumped when you scratched them, broke if you accidentally stepped on them, or warped when they got warm. On BBC TV's premier science programme, *Tomorrow's World*, presenter Judith Hann scratched one side of a CD to pieces with wire wool, and it still played perfectly. They even drilled a quarter-inch hole in a CD – and still it worked fine. "Astonishing!" the viewer was supposed to think. And because, unlike the old record player, there was no physical contact between a needle and the disc, the CD would never wear out. The compact disc seemed like a modern miracle!

A few facts about CDs

MAKE A NOTE!

An audio CD holds up to 74 minutes of sound which can be in as many as 99 tracks, but each track must start and end with two seconds of silence.

If you were to take the spiral of data on a CD and stretch it out into a single line, it would be over three miles in length!

A CD spins at a rate of between 250 and 500 revolutions per minute (rpm).

The speed at which a CD rotates is variable – faster when the laser is reading data from the middle of the disc where the circumference of the track is smaller, and slower when reading from the outside, so as to keep the 'linear speed' (at which the data passes under the laser) constant. The linear speed is between 1.2 and 1.4 metres per second.

A CD is 120mm in diameter, which is just under four-and three-quarter inches.

It's expensive, but it sounds amazing

The problem that Philips's marketing people had to overcome was that when they first came out CD players were pretty expensive – and the CDs themselves were shockingly dear, costing about £15 for the latest albums at a time when most people were paying about £6 for the same music on vinyl. At the time, anything over £10 seemed like an enormous amount to pay for music.

This is where the sound quality angle came in. Philips hoped that a hard core of 'early adopters' who were hi-fi buffs would scramble to try out the new, superior sound reproduction of CD players, and would influence the rest of the market to follow. Which is pretty much what happened.

Strangely, though, it's widely accepted that a single group – Dire Straits – became the key to the success of CD. The wealthy yuppie fans of the group could afford the expensive CD players and discs and were the sort of people for whom the production quality was as important as the music. They rushed out to buy new hi-fi systems on which to hear the albums *Love Over Gold* and *Brothers in Arms* at maximum quality, and with this boost in its target audience, the CD marketplace suddenly became big enough to ensure that compact disc would succeed.

It's a lesson, incidentally, that all technology manufacturers are aware of. The desirability of the software always leads the take-up of the hardware, it is said: which is why Sky satellite television was desperate to get hold of Premiership soccer coverage, and so boost the sales of satellite dishes.

Why compact disc is only human...

Perhaps the most peculiar thing about the success of CD is that we now know that all the things they said about it aren't exactly true.

Sure, you can drill a quarter-inch hole in a CD and it should still play fine, because error-checking code is included in the digital data, and this can make up for tiny gaps in the flow of sound. But as all CD owners will know, tiny scratches, or fingermarks, or bits of dust can all make a CD jump horribly.

Further, many early CD pressings have proven to have manufacturing faults that mean the plastic slowly disintegrates. And many hi-fi buffs, especially classical music fans, accuse the sound of a CD of being somewhat harsh, tinny or clinical, as opposed to the 'warm' sound of vinyl albums.

On top of all that, there are still massive arguments – not to mention Monopolies Commission reports and court cases – about whether CD music is overpriced, which all comes down to that ever-so-convenient commercial relationship that Philips established with music publishers to make sure CD would succeed.

Still, CD has proven its convenience and value. Whatever you think of CD music, the compact disc has one enormous advantage that has now taken it far beyond the realm of audio, and that's that it is a digital medium. Which is what has made CD-ROM possible, and will continue to open up some amazing possibilities.

Before we go any further, however, it would be useful to understand how a compact disc player works, and we'll start with digital sound.

Understanding how digital audio works, and PC sound cards

This is not essential to your understanding of CD-ROMs, so skip it if you wish, but while we're talking about how CDs work we might as well have a quick look at the way digital sound and music works.

It's not purely for casual interest, since one important part of a multimedia PC set-up is the sound card, and an understanding of how digital sound works will help you understand the technical terms used to describe the performance of a PC sound card, which will help you choose when you're buying. Incidentally, almost all PC sound cards come with sound sampling software that will enable you to play around with creating your own digital 'sampled' sounds, so there's a lot of fun to be had here as well.

How analogue sound recording works

Digital sound isn't better because it sounds any better. When you're listening, there really shouldn't be any discernible difference between digital sound, of the kind CDs use, and the sound created by an older, 'analogue' audio format. In fact, the challenge for digital sound is to get as close as possible to reproducing analogue sound.

That's because digital sound is made up of numbers – digital data that represents a description of the sound – whereas analogue sound is a direct representation of the sound itself. If that sounds a little confusing, don't fret, because it's really quite simple. It works like this.

As you no doubt already know, the best way of envisioning how sound works is to imagine it as a wave. The more high-pitched the sound, the higher the frequency of the wave (or, in other words, the peaks of the waves are closer together). The lower the pitch of the sound, the lower the frequency of the wave.

Musical instruments create waves of sound in the air by creating vibrations, whether it's the vibrating strings of a guitar or violin, or the vibrations caused by the passage of the air through a wind instrument like a flute. When it comes to playing recorded music from an electronic hi-fi, the waves in the air are caused by the vibrating of a loudspeaker cone, which is vibrated by an oscillating magnet, and the oscillations in the magnet are caused by a changing current of electricity.

When sound is being recorded, the way the microphone works is more or less an exact opposite of the loudspeaker. Set up a microphone in front of a musical instrument, and the vibrations of the air caused by the instrument make a diaphragm inside the microphone vibrate. The diaphragm in the microphone has a magnet attached, and the oscillation of the magnet causes an electrical current. And it's this changing electrical current which is recorded by a tape recorder.

WHAT DOES IT MEAN?

A tape recording is an 'analogue' recording, because the electrical impulses on the tape are directly analogous to the original vibrations, almost as if they were a miniature sculpture in electrical form of the original vibrations in the air.

Similarly, a vinyl record is also an analogue recording, because the grooves of the record contain a pattern of bumps and dips which exactly model the vibrations in the air that the microphone originally recorded.

A simple description of how digital sound works

The easiest way to picture how digital sound recordings are made is to visualise again the original sound wave, and imagine it drawn across a piece of graph paper. All you then have to do is move across the graph paper a millimetre at a time, checking at each point how high the sound wave is and writing the height of the wave down as a number.

WHAT DOES IT MEAN?

Effectively, that's what digital sound is: a series of numbers that represent the sound wave.

This process is actually carried out by a piece of electronics known as a an analogue to digital converter (known for short as an A-to-D converter). Rather than checking the height of the sound wave every millimetre on a sheet of graph paper, the A-to-D converter has an electronic signal fed into it from a microphone or a tape recording, and checks it 44,000 times every second. Each measurement is noted as a digital number – a number, that is, in the form of binary 1s and 0s. The digital sound recording system then records all these numbers, and there it is: you have you have your digital recording.

Sampling rates

This process of slicing the sound up, which the A-to-D converter carries out, is what's known as sampling. The frequency of the sampling operation – 44,000 times a second, or 44kHz (kiloHertz) – is known as the sampling rate.

The sampling rate used by CD players is quite a high one, and that's important to the quality of the sound. Many computer games – and also many other kinds of CD-ROM software, such as encyclopedias with music or speech on them – also use sampled sound, but it's very often at a lower sampling rate which means the quality of the sound is not as crisp and clear as genuine CD audio.

The figure of 44kHz is chosen because of the different frequencies of sound which the human ear can distinguish. If your ears are pretty good, you will be able to hear bass sounds that have a frequency as low as 20Hz, and treble sounds which have a frequency up to about 20kHz, though most people can't hear sounds that high. You'll very often see figures like this used to advertise the frequency response of headphones, for example. The sample rate needs to be twice the frequency of the highest-pitched sound, so the 44kHz frequency allows for sounds up to 22kHz to be digitised with accuracy.

Sound resolution

Sampled sound can be thought of in the same way as printed pictures. Newspaper pictures, for example, are made up of lots of tiny dots. If you have more, smaller dots, the picture will look clearer and sharper. The same thing applies to computer pictures, which as no doubt you're already aware, are made up of lots of tiny blocks called pixels. If you have more, smaller pixels on the screen, the picture will look clearer and sharper, which is why for displaying photographs on a PC screen, a higher resolution such as 800-by-600 pixels (that's 800 pixels across the screen, and 600 down) gives a clearer image.

With digital audio, however, the term 'resolution' has a different meaning. As we've already said, the A-to-D converter notes the size of the sound wave 44,000 times a second, and each time it does so, it records the size of the sound wave as a binary number.

WHAT DOES IT MEAN?

The 'resolution' of the sound has to do with how big this number is allowed to be. In fact, CD recordings use a sound resolution of 16 bits. A bit is a binary digit – a 1 or 0 – so this means that each of the numbers is made up of 16 binary 1s or 0s. And that means that each of the numbers could be anything from 0 to 65,535.

This figure represents the amplitude of the sound wave, and is considered to be of sufficient quality to reproduce sounds with the greatest possible clarity. Most modern sound cards are also 16-bit, though some older models have only an 8-bit resolution.

How the CD-DA audio standard works

As part of their efforts to ensure that audio CDs would become a worldwide standard, Sony and Philips set out a careful specification for the way CD data should be organised, and published it in a document which has come to be known as the Red Book. Part of the reason for this careful specification is that an audio CD includes lots of extra data over and above the actual music data.

The data is organised into short chunks known as sectors, each of which is 1/75th of a second long. As well as the binary data that represents the music, each sector also has extra data known as Error Detection and Error Correction Code (EDC and ECC). This enables the CD player to make up for gaps in the data – such as the gaps caused by the famous experiment of drilling a quarter-inch hole in the disc, as well as skips caused by dust and scratches – by looking at the ECC and EDC code and using it to reconstruct whatever is missing.

Each sector of data also includes timing codes, which are used by the CD player to keep track of elapsed track times.

The advantages of digital sound

Because a digital sound is simply a mathematical reconstruction of a real, analogue sound, it doesn't have any inherent magical qualities that make it in any way 'better'. All sound recordings have to be carefully balanced and 'equalised' in the studio before they can be reproduced, and the conditions imposed by the hi-fi they are played on, and the environment in which that hi-fi is situated, all have an enormous effect on the the final sound of a piece of recorded music. There are, however, two major advantages to digital music.

MAKE A NOTE!

The first is that when it is being sent down a wire in electronic form, digital data is not susceptible to picking up noise or interference.

Because all that's being sent and received at either end of the wire is 1s and 0s, there's simply no room for error. By contrast, an analogue signal in a wire is composed of all sorts of fluctuating levels of voltage, and can easily be distorted by electromagnetic interference and the properties of the wire itself. And if the flow of data in a digital signal is interrupted, the EDC and ECC checks can make up for the missing bits, while if analogue data is lost, it stays lost.

MAKE A NOTE!

The second advantage of digital sound is that it should not suffer any loss in quality when reproduced, for almost exactly the same reasons that it doesn't suffer loss in quality when transmitted down a wire.

Sony's original digital recording system, DAT (it stands for Digital Audio Tape), has been popular in professional use but was always too expensive for home use. Equally, the two digital recording systems aimed at home users – Sony's MiniDisc and Philips's Digital Compact Cassette – are still very expensive.

They are, however, guaranteed to give 100% perfect copies of whatever they record: because all that goes on the tape is 1s and 0s, so the recording is not susceptible to deterioration from variations the way an electrical signal would be. In theory, you could make a copy of a CD on a digital tape, then make a copy of the copy, and then a copy of the copy of the copy… and go on as many times as you wish, each time with absolutely no loss in quality whatsoever.

Digital recording studios

Until recently, the actual recording of music has remained an analogue process, recording to one-inch studio tape. The music would be later digitised in to a digital system to create a digital master from which CDs would be produced.

Inevitably, though, the technology has now been developed whereby the whole recording process can be made digital. German classical music specialists Deutsche Grammophon, for example, published their first all-digital recordings in October 1993. The recordings were made at DG's Hanover studios where the very first process in the recording chain is to digitise the sound, and a 21-bit sound resolution is used throughout to ensure the maximum sound quality: though the finished result is still a standard 16-bit-resolution CD.

How CDs are made

Probably the most surprising thing about a compact disc is that, just like an old-fashioned vinyl album, the finished thing is stamped out of plastic. Anyway, here's a very brief run-through of the process.

First, a master is made on a mastering lathe, and powerful laser is used to expose an image on the blank master. This disc is then developed and electroplated, and used to create a press stamper made out of pure nickel.

The press stamper is then used in conjunction with an injection-moulding machine to stamp out the copies of the CD from clear plastic. The bottom of the disc is then coated with an ultra-thin layer of metal, and the whole thing is covered with a layer of clear lacquer to protect it.

The whole of the production process must be carried out in an ultra-clean, dust-free 'safe' environment: each bit of data is represented by an area of less than a thousandth of a millimetre on the surface of the disc, and a single particle of household dust could destroy many Kilobytes of data.

How the CD player works

The mechanism inside a CD-ROM drive is exactly the same, and works in exactly the same way, as the mechanism inside an audio CD player.

In fact, the CD-ROM drives you buy are usually based around an off-the-shelf CD player mechanism, and drives are made by the exact same electronics firms – Sony, Matsushita, Panasonic, JVC and so on – who make CD players, and that's for the simple reason that the two are exactly the same. The only difference is that a CD-ROM drive is under the overall control of your computer, whereas the CD player is under the control of pre-programmed microchips inside the CD player.

The workings of a CD player are essentially very simple. There's a mechanism to spin the disc, a laser attached to a moving 'read head' which can scan across the surface of the disc in a straight line, and a photo-electric cell which picks up laser light reflected from the surface of the disc and converts it into electrical impulses.

A compact disc is 120mm in diameter, which is almost exactly four-and-three-quarter inches. The data on the CD is recorded, as is appropriate for binary information, as a series of 'on' and 'off' impulses. These are represented respectively by indentations in the surface of the disc known as 'pits' and flat areas, known as 'lands'.

A laser is used for two reasons: one, the beam of light it produces is very tightly focussed, actually smaller than the point of a needle; two, the beam of light has exactly parallel sides, so there is a vastly reduced chance of any light scattering.

As the CD spins, the laser is aimed at it and deflected by the pits on the disc, flicking the beam of light onto the photoelectric cell, which converts the flashes of light into impulses of electricity (various prisms and mirrors are used along the way, to deflect the beam of light in the right direction and stop it scattering, but really they don't come in to the equation). It's actually a terribly simple mechanism, which is one of its great advantages, and of course there is no physical contact with the disc, which is why CDs are theoretically not prone to wearing in the same way a vinyl LP is.

There is one slight complication, which is that the disc has to be spun at a variable speed – slower when the laser read head is towards the outside of the disc, and faster when it's near the middle. That's because, obviously enough, at the middle of the disc one complete revolution of the disc only covers a short distance, and therefore represents only a small amount of data; whereas at the outside edge of the disc, one complete revolution covers a much greater distance, and therefore represents a much larger amount of data.

In order to make the whole thing work, the speed at which data is travelling past the laser read head must be kept constant: and so the disc rotates much more slowly when the laser is at the outside edge of the disc, and gradually accelerates as it moves towards the centre of the disc. And so the 'linear speed' – the speed at which the data would be travelling if it were stretched out in one single line, instead of wrapped in a spiral on a disc – remains constant.

The linear speed at which data passes under the laser (or 'over' the laser, really, since the data is always on the bottom of the CD) is between 1.2 and 1.4 metres per second, and the disc can spin at speeds from 250rpm to 500rpm. And if you were able stretch out the spiral of data on a CD into a single line, it would be about three miles long!

Variable speeds and floppy disks

Incidentally, it might interest you to know that the floppy disk drives used in Macintosh computers also use a variable-speed mechanism, for a similar reason. Apple wished to keep the linear speed at which data passed under the magnetic read head of the floppy disk drive constant. Because Apple drives are made this way, it's much easier for Apple machines to read disks in a PC format than it is for a PC to read Mac disks – the PC disk drive can't be forced to run at variable speeds.

Caring for CDs

As we've already pointed out, CDs are not the miracle medium that they might have seemed when they first appeared. Small scratches on the surface of the disc can easily deflect the laser beam, and so cause the disc to skip: which is nuisance enough on a music album, but can easily render a CD-ROM disc completely useless.

For that reason, it's important to look after your CDs very carefully. Treat them with kid gloves. Here are some basic rules that might help.

WARNING

1. Always put CDs back in a proper CD case after using them. This will protect them from dust and scratches.

2. If you really insist on leaving a CD outside its case, always put it down with the side with the label printed on it downwards. CDs are single-sided and the data is read only from the bottom, so that's where scratches matter: the side with a label printed on is of no great importance.

3. Always handle CDs carefully by just catching them between your fingers, with the extreme edges resting against your fingers, or hold them with a finger through the hole in the middle. Never hold a CD with a 'pinch'-style action. Fingermarks can easily make a CD skip.

4. To clean a CD, use a very soft cloth – paper tissues are actually far too harsh and scratchy. Wipe them with an action moving from the centre of the disc to the outside: if you move in circles around the disc, any minute scratches you might make will be too similar to the direction of the spiral of data on the disc, and so the laser might pick them up.

5. You can actually wash CDs in water quite happily, but never use a solvent to clean them because this can eat into or cloud the lacquer that covers the disc. If you need to give a disc a really good clean, buy special CD cleaners – these do not contain harmful solvents.

6. Make sure your disc boxes (or 'jewel cases' as they're known, for the simple reason that the marketing industry thinks the clear plastic is jewel-like – ho hum) are in good condition, and especially the 'sprocket' onto which the CD clips. The sprocket is intended to hold the disc away from the surface of the disc box, and if it's broken or collapsed, the underside of the disc will scrape against the bottom of the case, and may get scratched.

7. Always take your discs out of the jewel case in the approved manner! It may sound silly, but there is a right way of 'using' a CD box that not everyone knows, and if you do it the right way, your cases are less likely to get broken and your CDs are less likely to get scratched. We've got

instructions on how to use a CD case for you right here on these pages...

8. If a CD does get slightly scratched, you may find that you can fix it using a CD repair kit, available in most hi-fi shops. The kit comprises a bottle of lacquer and a soft cloth, and you can use the lacquer to coat the disc so that it fills in the scratches, smoothing them out so that they are no longer picked up by the laser.

How to use a CD case (yes, seriously!)

OK, as we've already mentioned, there is a right way of opening a CD case and taking the CD out. Please don't be insulted if you know this already, but many people really have no idea about this, and spend their whole lives wondering why their CD cases are prone to flying apart at the hinges, sending their discs bouncing around the room. If you use the approved method, you should be able to avoid ever breaking a CD case again, and also be able to prolong the life of your CDs. Incidentally, I've written the instructions assuming you're right-handed, not out of any sinister prejudice but because I am right-handed myself.

1. Opening the box

Notice that there are little 'half moon' shapes on the top and bottom edges of the CD case, at the end away from the hinge. These are pressure points which, when you press them, release the clips inside the case. So...

a) Let the disc case rest flat on the palm of your right hand, with your fingers holding the back edge (the hinge end) and your thumb holding the front edge (the end that opens).

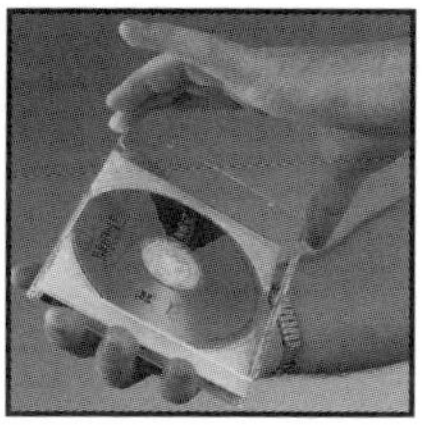

b) Put the thumb and forefinger of your left hand on the pressure points at the top and bottom edges of the CD case, right over by your right thumb.

c) Press gently with the thumb and forefinger of your left hand, and you should find the clips are released and it's easy to unhinge the top of the case without the whole thing springing out of your hands.

2. Taking out the CD

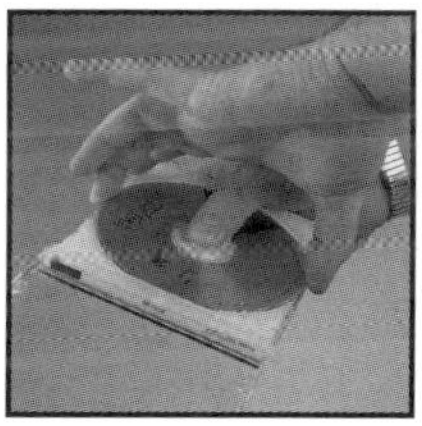

a) Let the CD case rest open in your right hand, and depress the sprocket holding the disc in the case with the index finger of your left hand. The disc should now come loose from its casing.

b) Now place your thumb (at the bottom) and your forefinger (at the top) of your left hand on the very edges of the CD, and lift it free of the jewel case. Handling the disc by its outer rim only will prevent any fingerprints or debris from your hands getting on the disc.

Chapter 3
The CD-ROM drive

- A brief history of CD-ROM
- CD-ROM discs and formats
- CD-ROM drives explained

A CD-ROM drive like this Sony double speed CDU31A is the key component in a multimedia computer system. but how does it work, and what should you look for when buying one? It's all explained in this chapter. Read on...

Introduction

In the last chapter, we looked at the development of audio CDs and the basics of how a CD player works, which is essentially exactly the same as a CD-ROM drive. In this chapter, it's time to get down to the nitty gritty of CD-ROM drives and CD formats.

First we'll look at all the factors which will help you understand what you're getting when you buy a CD-ROM drive. The adverts are full of technical terms and figures – things like drive speeds, seek times and caches – which at first seem pretty confusing but are actually very simple, so don't worry about those.

Then we'll have a look at disc formats. You'll notice terms like ISO9660 and CD-ROM X/A cropping up a lot, but there's really nothing to them, so we'll get those sorted out too.

What does 'CD-ROM' stand for?

WHAT DOES IT MEAN?

The term CD-ROM stands for 'Compact Disc Read-Only Memory', the derivation of the name being that a CD is storage for data – and therefore, in general computer terms, 'memory' – but a disc is printed by a manufacturer, and can not be altered by the user, and is therefore a 'read-only' medium.

Compare that with hard disk drives, for instance, which are known as 'Read/Write' media, and the recent development of writeable CDs, which are often called 'WORM' – Write Once, Read Many times – drives because the user can store data in the first place but cannot alter it later. We'll be taking a look at writeable CDs, which are more usually known as CD-R or 'CD-Recordable', later in this book.

The CD-ROM standard

After CD audio had been invented, inevitably it was quickly realised that the digital format used by the discs could be adapted to storing digital computer data, and so Sony and Philips started work on a new format soon after the original 'Red Book' standard for CD Digital Audio (or CD-DA as we'll refer to it from now on) was published.

The early CD-ROM standard was established a long time ago in computer terms and it was published in a document known as the 'Yellow Book'.

One of the basic ideas was that a CD-ROM could be a 'mixed mode' disc, with standard CD-DA audio tracks on it as well, so the normal CD audio standard formed the basis for the new computer standard. The designers then also added two new types of track, known as CD-ROM Mode 1 and CD-ROM Mode 2.

Mode 1 was designed purely for normal computer data, while Mode 2 was intended for compressed audio and for video data. Both Modes had extra data over and above that used on audio tracks. Mode 1 also added an extra, third level of error detection and correction code (EDC and ECC) on top of the two layers that were already used by CD-DA audio. Mode 2 held more data, but with less error correction.

So CD-ROM discs could, potentially, contain both audio and computer tracks. Because the CD-ROM drive mechanism is exactly the same as a CD player mechanism, there's no reason why they shouldn't. And they do. Incidentally, if you have a CD-ROM disc with CD-DA audio tracks on it, there's no reason why you can't play the audio tracks on a normal CD player: The only problem will be that older CD players, which aren't equipped to cut out the computer data tracks, will try to play the computer data: it makes a horrible racket, rather like a fax machine sounds when you call one by accident on a phone line.

The advantage of the new CD-ROM format, however, was that it could store massive amounts of data – the equivalent of 100,000 A4 pages of text was the favourite way of putting it at the time.

A (very) brief history of CD-ROM

Applications for CD-ROM were somewhat slow to take off, and were mainly technical or scientific in nature. In its early days, the CD-ROM drive was a serious tool for serious people. By the beginning of 1989, there were about 100,000 CD-ROM drives in use around the world, most of them attached to PCs, with just a few adapted for use on Apple Macintosh computers (probably only about 5,000 worldwide).

However, the computer entertainment market was beginning to take a strong interest in CD-ROM. In Japan, NEC were preparing to release a version of their PC Engine games console which housed a CD-ROM drive instead of the normal slot for cartridges. Meanwhile, Philips and Sony were working on the Compact Disc Interactive (CD-i) system, which was to be a home entertainment system based around CD-ROM and the rival Digital Video Interactive, based on add-on cards for a PC (and similar in approach to the current Video CD standard) was being worked on.

More importantly, two significant CD-ROM 'games' had just been published. UK games software publisher Mirrorsoft, which later disappeared when Robert Maxwell did the same, released the first real CD-ROM game for the PC in mid-1989. It was an adaptation of the successful Cinemaware production *Defender of the Crown*, with lots of added CD-DA sound and music to spice it up, as well as added animation.

At the beginning of 1989 US publisher Activision released The *Manhole* for Apple Mac CD-ROM. It was created by the team who went on to produce the amazing adventure game Myst for

Broderbund. The Manhole was an 'interactive adventure' for children, and set the pattern for much of the best children's multimedia software which followed.

At the same time the print publishing world was taking an interest in CD-ROM, seeing the potential it had as a new way of creating books. It started with newspapers like the *Times* and the *Guardian*, who published annual collections on CD-ROM of a whole year's worth of newspaper text, which made an ideal research resource for libraries.

Over the next couple of years, certain enlightened publishers led the way in exploring the new medium. Hutchinson's in England worked on an interactive version of their encyclopedia, but much of the running was made by American firms such as Time Warner, who set up the Warner New Media division to explore all kinds of new formats, Compton's, who also saw the encyclopedia angle as a good bet, Discis, who published children's picture books and Xiphias, with a whole range of reference works including cookery books and their '*Timetable of...*' series.

Most of what was published was for PC CD-ROM. And the public was slow to buy CD-ROM drives, so the market wasn't big enough for any profits to be made. The publishers were nevertheless willing to invest money in developing expertise which they were sure would later stand them in good stead.

The breakthrough for CD-ROM came only very recently, and was due to several factors. For starters, the number of CD-ROM drives in circulation finally reached a level where it became economically viable for publishers to create CD-ROM titles. Moreover, it became widely accepted in the computer entertainment industry that CD-ROMs were a cheaper, more efficient way of distributing software than either floppy disks or video game cartridges.

Secondly, the older single-speed CD-ROM drives were overtaken by newer double-speed drives (we'll explain that shortly), which were capable of running much more spectacular applications, including the video clips which became a major selling point for CDd software. Shortly afterwards, the selling price of CD-ROM drives came down dramatically, from around £400 a unit to as little as £150.

Probably the crucial factor, though, was that certain key titles were published that made people want to buy CD-ROM drives just to use them. Among them were the Virgin game *The 7th Guest*, which caused an enormous stir in 1993, and Microsoft's *Encarta* encyclopedia, which was suddenly reduced in price from about £250 to less than £90.

So it was that in 1993 the number of CD-ROM drives in circulation reached a critical mass, and the whole thing exploded. CD-ROM is now seen as the most important publishing medium by most of the computer leisure industry, and sales of encyclopedias on CD-ROM are said to outsell normal printed versions. And, hopefully, the best is yet to come...

Choosing a CD-ROM drive

Before we go any further, we might as well run through what to look for when buying a CD-ROM drive – and along the way we'll also look at a few of the key terms and functions of a CD-ROM drive.

Within certain limits, most CD-ROM drives are pretty much the same, and so you're free to buy on price. The main thing that varies is the build quality, but you're unlikely to see a CD-ROM drive that's so badly made that it would fall apart in use. (Some of the earlier Sony CD-ROM drives had a rather crude mechanism for the flip-out tray which acted a bit like a catapult, slinging discs across the room, but Sony have recently completely updated their range.)

One of the most popular CD-ROM drives for the PC is the Panasonic CD-562. It's as quick as you need, and its also very good value at about £150.

We've got some advice about specific models of CD-ROM drive for you later in this chapter, but we'll start with a run-through of the capabilities of a CD-ROM drive, and what to look for.

Incidentally, one thing we have avoided mentioning for the time being – it's dealt with in a later chapter – is the MPC and MPC2 standards, which you'll often see mentioned as a feature of a CD-ROM drive in an advertisement. 'MPC2 compliant', the ad might boast. Basically all you need to know for now is that it's a standard that covers the speed (both data transfer rate and seek time) of a CD-ROM drive.

As we've said, CD-ROM drives are all pretty similar, so long as you follow the basic advice – get a double-speed CD-ROM XA drive which has Photo CD multi-session capability. All this is explained below. In fact the main consideration when you're buying a CD-ROM drive for a PC is not the CD-ROM drive itself, but the method of connecting it up, so take careful note of the details about interfaces.

About CD-ROM drives: drive speeds

The 'speed' of a CD-ROM drive is a measure of how quickly it can transfer data. The basic standard against which drives are measured is set by the

audio CD player, which can transfer data at a rate of approximately 150 Kilobytes per second (150K/sec).

Single and double speeds

The transfer rate of 150K/sec was usual for CD-ROM drives until quite recently, and is referred to as 'single-speed'. More recently, drives have been created which can spin the disc twice as quickly, and so transfer data much faster. These are 'double-speed' drives, which transfer data at a rate of around 300K/sec, though some are actually slightly faster that that.

Double-speed drives are now pretty much the minimum standard, and when buying a CD-ROM drive you are strongly advised to buy a double-speed drive. Although you can still buy single-speed CD-ROM drives (and they're often very cheap), they're not worth the money because they're not up to the job – unless you have the most basic of needs, and only want to access text from reference CDs.

The reason why most of us will find a single-speed drive inadequate is that the transfer of large quantities of data such as photographs will be noticeably slow. And, more especially, that single-speed drives are not quick enough to provide a constant flow of large amounts of data, which is what you need to be able to run video clips.

One problem that affects all CD-ROM drives – even double-speed drives – is that they are much slower at transferring data to the computer than hard disk drives are. This makes the limitations of a single-speed drive especially noticeable.

Triple and quad-speed drives

Thanks to the latest technical innovations, you can now also buy CD-ROM drives that transfer data at three times the rate of a single-speed drive (triple-speed) or even four times the speed (quad-speed drives). Great stuff, and highly desirable. But there is one small drawback.

The trouble is that the normal red laser used in a CD player or CD-ROM drive is not sufficiently tightly focused to use in a CD-ROM drive that's running at three or four times the standard speed. Instead, these drives must use a different kind of laser (blue light). This makes them substantially more expensive to manufacture.

If money is no problem to you, then by all means go for a quad-speed, six-disc Pioneer 604X, but at £1,280 it's going to cost as much as a decent 486 PC.

Access times (seek times)

There is one other important factor that affects the speed of a CD-ROM drive, and that's how long it takes to find a particular item on the disc. This is called the 'seek time' or 'access time'.

As you can well imagine, when a CD player is playing an audio CD it usually starts at the beginning and moves through to the end, so how fast it can skip back and forth from one place on the disc to another is barely a factor. With a CD-ROM, however, you are constantly making choices about which piece of data you want the software to access next, and so the laser read head is constantly skipping around the disc, trying to find the data you want.

You might not think it would make a great deal of difference, but CD-ROMs are much slower at finding a particular piece of data than hard disk drives are, and it does become painfully apparent when you have to wait for the drive to find your data. So look for a CD-ROM drive with as fast an access time (or 'seek time') as possible.

Access times are measured as an average, because while you're using a CD, the laser read head might sometimes have to skip a very long way across the disc, and at other times it might have to make only a very short jump.

The usual figure quoted is for a 'one-third stroke' seek time, the stroke being the entire distance from the outside edge of the CD to the middle. The average length of the journey your laser read head will have to make to find the piece of data you want is one third of the stroke distance, so that is taken as the average measurement. You will also occasionally see 'full stroke' seek times quoted as well.

An average performance for a decent CD-ROM drive will be a one-third stroke time of 350 milliseconds (350ms), with the full stroke at about 650ms. Anything faster than that is good, and a one-third stroke seek time of 300ms or faster is very good indeed.

Caches for extra speed

MAKE A NOTE!

One piece of trickery that can be used either by your CD-ROM drive or by your computer in order to speed up the access of data is the use of a cache, also known as a 'data buffer'.

A cache is simply a piece of RAM memory (memory on a chip that can be filled and emptied very rapidly) which is used to temporarily store data on its way from the CD-ROM drive to the main RAM inside the computer. The CD-ROM drive can load data into the cache slightly before it's needed by the computer, so that when the computer comes to look for it, the data is already in the cache, from which it can be taken very rapidly. This speeds up the access of data, and also smooths out the flow of data.

Many CD-ROM drives are fitted with an internal RAM cache, which might seem small when you compare it with the RAM used by the computer, but will nevertheless help speed up your CD-ROM drive. A typical cache might be only 64K, but it's still effective. The larger the cache is, the more effective it will be.

An alternative is the use of a caching utility on the computer that's powering the CD-ROM drive, and there are quite a few programs of this type available for PC-compatible computers, besides the Smartdrv option which is built in to recent versions of MS-DOS. Caching utilities set aside an area of the computer's main RAM memory to be used as a cache for either hard disk drives or CD-ROM drives. The only problem is that some CD-ROM software, especially games, will not work when the caching utility is in operation, so you need to understand how to set up your PC's memory using different autoexec.bat configurations.

The Apple Macintosh, incidentally, uses a permanent disk cache, the size of which can be set using the Memory panel in the Control Panels folder (System 7 and above).

About CD-ROM drives: types and standards

There are a number of different standards whose names you will come across when choosing a CD-ROM drive, as follows.

- **CD-ROM XA compatible**
- **Kodak Photo CD ready**
- **Multi-session capable**

Essentially, there's no problem at all about these, because they're all things that all modern CD-ROM drives will have and you should buy a CD-ROM drive that has the lot. But here's a brief explanation of what they are.

CD-ROM XA

WHAT DOES IT MEAN?

This stands for CD-ROM Extended Architecture, and is a variation on the original Yellow Book CD-ROM standard.

Essentially, what happened was that it became apparent that the CD-ROM Mode 2 part of the original CD-ROM standard was not being used by anyone, so some bunch of bright sparks set about the process of coming up with a new, more useful variation of Mode 2 which would be called Mode 2 XA.

One addition is a 'data subheader' which can be used to describe the data in each sector, but more importantly, Mode 2 XA can combine audio and computer data so that it is 'interleaved'. All this really means is that short pieces of audio data can be slipped in between the pieces of computer data: it can then be constantly read back off the disc, in a way that effectively means simultaneous playing of computer data and audio. In other words, it means you can listen to a piece of music even while the computer is loading something.

The audio data can be run at two different levels of compression, compared to normal CD-DA sound – Level B compression, which is of a sufficient quality to play music, would give five hours of stereo or ten hours of mono sound on a disc, while Level C compression, of a lower quality suitable only for speech, would give ten hours of stereo speech and twenty of mono.

One of the main effects of this new standard is that it is now possible to play video clips from CD-ROM XA discs, which is what led to the development of the QuickTime (Apple Macintosh) and Video for Windows (PC-compatible) video standards. With the video and soundtrack interleaved, the two remain in perfect synchronisation.

The most important thing to know about CD-ROM XA, however, is that it requires extra hardware in the CD-ROM drive to decode the

Gold coloured Photo CD discs are recordable CD-ROMs that contain digitised photographs. To use them, your CD-ROM drive must support CD-ROM XA and multi-session.

interleaved data in the Mode 2 sectors. For this reason, some older CD-ROM drives cannot play discs that use CD ROM XA formats, and when you are buying a CD-ROM drive you should ensure that it is CD-ROM XA compatible. All new CD-ROM drives are OK.

Kodak Photo CD

This is dealt with in greater detail in a later chapter, but basically Photo CD is a system developed by Kodak that means you can pop down to your local photo shop or Boots the Chemist and have your photographs (slides or negatives) scanned and put on a CD-ROM disc.

If you have a special Photo CD player you can then watch your photos as a slideshow on your TV. But with a normal CD-ROM drive attached to a computer you can not only display Photo CD pictures on your monitor screen, but also pull them off the CD-ROM and onto your hard drive so that you can include them in DTP documents.

The important thing to note, however, is that Photo CD uses the same CD-ROM XA standard (apparently, part of the reason for this is that Kodak plan to add music and narration to later versions of Photo CD). There are two points to this. The first is that Photo CD capability is pretty useful and well worth exploring, and the second is that 'Photo CD Ready' or 'Photo CD compatible' is another way of saying a CD-ROM drive is CD-ROM XA standard, so look out for it on adverts and make sure you get a Photo CD compatible drive.

Multi-session

Once upon a time, there would be only one set of data on a CD-ROM disc. At the start of the disc is a Table of Contents (ToC) which describes all the data on the disc. It's used for things like indicating the total running time on audio CDs, and for an index of where data is on a CD-ROM disc. The original CD-ROM standard allowed for only one ToC.

However, the next thing that happened was that writeable CD-R discs came along, and the need developed for users to be able to put one set of data on a disc originally, then add a second, or even third, set of data on a CD-ROM, space permitting, at a later date: which meant more ToCs.

The CD-ROM standard was adapted to be able to handle this, making sure that the CD-ROM drive would look for other ToCs if they existed. Since each time a new set of data is written on to a disc it is referred to as a 'session', these discs are referred to as 'multi-session' discs.

Obviously most CD-ROMs you buy will be single-session discs, but you do need to be able to handle multi-session discs. And again, Photo CD discs are also multi-session – if you have a disc with some pictures on and the disc isn't full, you can go back to Boots at a later date and have extra pictures put on it.

You'll often see the words 'multi-session' on a CD-ROM drive advertisement, usually alongside the Photo CD tag. Remember that you do want your CD-ROM drive to have multi-session support.

About CD-ROM drives: the caddy

One choice you might like to bear in mind is whether or not your CD-ROM drive uses a 'caddy' to hold CD-ROM discs.

A caddy is simply a cartridge or case, with a flip-up top, into which you put the CD-ROM disc. You then slide the whole caddy into the CD-ROM drive to use it. Apple CD-ROM drives use a caddy system, whereas the majority of PC CD-ROM drives don't – they tend to have a motorised tray, just like an audio CD player, which rolls out so that you can drop the CD onto it, then slides back inside the CD-ROM drive mechanism. So does it matter?

Well, the one big advantage of a caddy system is if you have a number of discs which are in constant use but are regularly swapped over. Typical situations might be in a library or a school environment. Here, the CD-ROM discs that are in frequent use can be left permanently in a caddy, which will protect them from dust and damage, even if they are frequently being swopped for other discs and left lying around on desks and tables. The only drawback is that the caddies themselves are relatively expensive, at about £5 each.

One variant on the caddy that can be useful for libraries in particular is the security caddy, which incorporates an electronic tag to prevent the disc from being removed from the library. There's a firm called Stralfors (0793 488008) which specialises in security caddies, and they even make a maximum-security version that explodes if it's opened by unauthorised personnel!

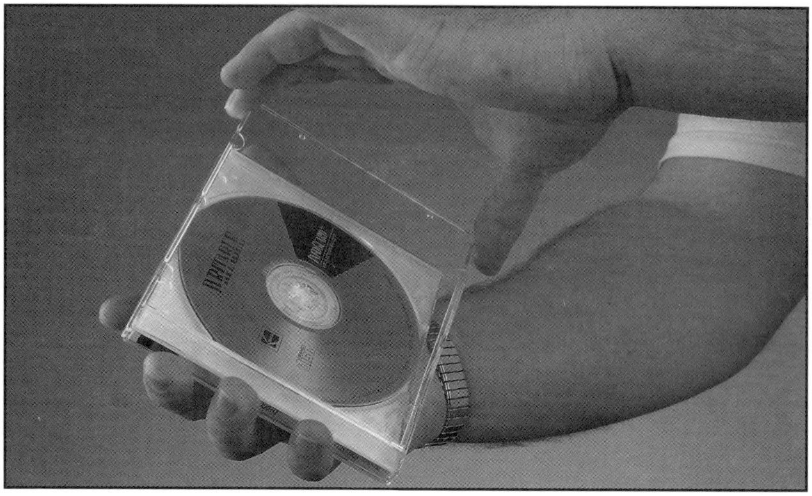

How to use a CD caddy properly!

Yes, it was bad enough being told about the right way to open a CD case, but it's also important that you do the right thing with a CD caddy, too. In particular, if you don't close the lid properly, you could get the caddy stuck in the CD-ROM drive – which could be embarrassing or expensive if you have to get someone to fix it for you!

1. Opening the caddy

It's important to notice that there are two sprung clips at the corners of the caddy. You must press these in while you open the lid. Then slip the CD-ROM disc into the caddy, dropping it in at the front end, where the hinge is, first.

2. Closing the caddy

This is the important bit. Make sure the CD-ROM disc is properly seated inside the caddy, then close the lid and be sure to press down at the corners, where the clips hold the lid shut. You should hear both clips click into place. If the lid isn't closed flat, the caddy will get stuck in the drive when you try to take it out. If there's a problem, it might be because the lid has come off the hinges at the other end, so keep an eye on that as well. While you're about it, it's worth turning the caddy over and making sure that the sliding metal shutter moves freely and will spring back into place.

About CD-ROM drives: the importance of interfaces

The CD-ROM drive in itself is going to do you no good at all unless you can hook it up to your computer and get the two talking to each other, and for that you need an 'interface'. The situation is rather different for PCs and Apple Macs, so we'll deal with the two cases separately.

Apple Macintosh CD-ROM drives

With the Mac, it's pretty straightforward because Mac CD-ROM drives all use the standard SCSI interface (it stands for Small Computer Systems Interface, and is pronounced 'scuzzy').

All Macs have a SCSI interface socket on the back, so it's pretty simple to hook your CD-ROM drive up to it. If you buy a new Mac with a CD-ROM drive ready fitted, the CD-ROM drive will be inside the computer. But if you're buying a CD-ROM drive to fit to a Mac you've got already, the drive will almost invariably be an external add-on in its own stand-alone case, which you fit just by plugging it in and placing it on the desk next to your Mac.

Which means you only have two small things to worry about. One, you want to make sure you get a SCSI interface cable when you buy your CD-ROM drive, preferably thrown in for free. And two, you'll need to check that you get a SCSI terminator to go on the back of the

CD-ROM drive. Because SCSI devices can be 'daisy chained' in a big, long string of hardware, the last device in the chain must always have a terminator plug on it to tell the computer that this is the end of the SCSI chain. Again, you should get this free with your CD-ROM drive.

One last thing to remember is that you should never plug in or disconnect hardware from your Mac while it is switched on. Even if you don't break anything, the Mac probably won't recognise the device until you restart it anyway. So shut down and switch off your Mac before you plug in a new CD-ROM drive.

PC CD-ROM drives

Generally, it's assumed that when you buy a CD-ROM drive for a PC, you will not already have an interface ready for it to be attached to.

You can fit a CD-ROM drive internally, inside the case of your PC, or externally, in its own case and attached to the PC by a cable. In both cases, the interface is far more than just the cable that connects the drive up. The most important part will be a hardware interface card fitted inside the PC.

SCSI interfaces: if you do already have an interface available, it's most likely to be a SCSI interface card (SCSI stands for Small Computer Systems Interface, and is pronounced 'scuzzy') which has been fitted as a hard disk drive controller. You can comfortably attach a CD-ROM drive to the SCSI interface and in fact this is often the simplest way of fitting a CD-ROM drive, but you will need to make sure when you buy the drive that it is SCSI or SCSI2 compatible (the newer SCSI2 system is faster, yet remains compatible with existing SCSI equipment) and that you get the necessary cables. If you need a sound card anyway, then getting a multimedia upgrade kit will most likely still be a better option.

Proprietary interfaces: this is probably the least cost-effective sort of interface to use. A proprietary interface is designed specifically to connect one make of CD-ROM drive to a PC, and so has no other function, which makes it less useful than the third option…

Sound card: in a good multimedia PC you'll want a good sound card anyway, so that you can hear the audio in full effect. Nearly all CD-ROM drives can use various popular models of sound card as an interface, so by buying a sound card you effectively get a free interface card at the same time. If you already have a sound card, just look for a CD-ROM drive that is compatible with it. If you don't already have a sound card, then your best bet will probably be to buy a multimedia upgrade kit.

Multimedia upgrade kits: an all-in-one kit will usually be much the best value. As well as a CD-ROM drive and a sound card which you can use as an interface for the drive, you'll generally also get a pair of powered stereo speakers so that you get the full impact of your sound card, as well as examples of free software (particularly free CD-ROM discs, the value of which can often add up to several times the price of the upgrade kit).

About CD-ROM drives: multiple CD use

Probably the only other consideration you'll need to bear in mind will be if you're buying a CD-ROM system for use in an educational or business environment where you may want a particular set of CD-ROM discs to be permanently available, perhaps on a network.

In this case you have two options. You can either buy a multi-disc changer drive (most changer drives will hold up to six discs), or you can buy a set of SCSI drives and chain them together. Inevitably, the six-disc changer model will be the cheaper option, because you're only paying for one drive mechanism.

Buying a CD-ROM drive: some specific models

There is a wide range of different CD-ROM drives on offer, not only as stand-alone purchases but also in upgrade kits and built in to ready-made multimedia PCs. Whichever way you're buying a CD-ROM drive, it will help to know what the reviewers thought of the make and model you're being offered, so here's a brief run-down of some that have been tested by Future Publishing's PC Plus and CD-ROM Today magazines.

All CD-ROM drives are made by well-known electronics manufacturers, partly because the mechanisms are exactly the same as the audio CD players that the same firms make. Because these are well-known firms, you can be pretty sure that what you're getting will be up to scratch. But because there's no real distinguishing factor to help you, the way the sound quality might if you were looking at hi-fi systems, the decision does tend to come down to price, and less tangible factors such as build quality.

One interesting figure which some manufacturers quote is mean time between breakdowns, but of course these figures are not independently tested.

What if you really can't decide what to get? Well, for Apple Macintosh owners, the choice is pretty simple because the AppleCD 300 is clearly your best bet. But for PC owners, the one the staff at CD-ROM Today tend to advise people to buy is a Panasonic double-speed model (562 or 563), which performs well in tests and yet is very good value, on sale for as little as £160.

To give you a better idea of what's on the market, here's a round-up of the more popular models.

Apple Macintosh CD-ROM drives

AppleCD 150: an older single-speed model named after its 150K/sec transfer rate. You might see this one on sale at bargain basement rates, but don't be tempted. I've tried running a Mac from a single-speed drive, and believe me, it's really not worth it.

Apple PowerCD: looks really unusual and interesting, this one, with its peculiar curved design. Intriguingly, it also acts as a stand-alone audio CD player or even Photo CD player, complete with zoom, which is great. And it has a remote control. But tragically, it's only a single-speed drive, which makes it painfully slow in use. And I wasn't too impressed by the build quality. If you want a Photo CD player that you can take around with you to show off the family snapshots on other people's TVs, you might be tempted, especially since the price has just been halved, so you can buy it for about £169. Contact: Freefone Apple.

AppleCD 300: this is the CD-ROM drive that just about everyone has. It's a decent price (about £175) for a decent performer (double-speed), and as a plug-in-and-go solution it's recommended. Contact: Freefone Apple.

PC CD-ROM drives

Hitachi 6700: a double-speed drive, but one that proved to be the slowest of six drives tested by PC Plus magazine. And it is really too expensive at £470 RRP. Its main advantages are a high build quality – it's a robust old thing – and the fact that it uses caddies, unlike most PC drives, which you might prefer. Hitachi have a wide range, though, with the newer 1950 and 6750 double-speed drives claiming faster transfer rates as well as great reliability. Contact Hitachi on 081 249 2092.

Orchid CDS3110: this double-speed drive is pretty good on transfer speeds, at about 300K/sec on test, but it falls down on slightly slow seek times. On the other hand it costs only £169, and is especially good value as part of an Orchid sound card bundle or multimedia upgrade kit. Contact Orchid on 0256 479898.

Panasonic CR562: another double-speed drive, with a decent transfer speed and seek time performance, and especially good value (it's usually the cheapest drive you can buy, at around £150). Widely fitted, popular and a good buy. Contact Panasonic on 0344 853282.

Mitsumi FX001: double-speed but capable of significantly quicker transfer speeds when tested (around 370K/sec) and pretty cheap at around £169, its only real drawback being a slightly less robust build. Still, a good option. Contact Mitsumi on 0276 29029.

Sony CDU31A: a double-speed drive which scored very well on data transfer rates (approaching 400K/sec on test) but was let down very badly by seek times which didn't reach the MPC2 standard, and by its cheap pop-out drawer which threatened to send CDs flying across the room. However, that's not the whole story. Sony have since released the new CDU33A with fully MPC2-compliant seek times and an RRP of only £195, which should mean it will appear on sale at as little as £150. Contact Sony on 0784 467000.

Pioneer DRM-604X: this is a bit of a star among CD-ROM drives, since it's not only a six-disc changer (you can put up to six CD-ROM discs in a magazine and the drive can swap between them) but also a quad-speed drive, giving it data transfer rates in excess of 500K/sec. Despite the £1,280 asking price it can represent good value in some situations, but if you can't afford it and you still want a six-disc changer, there's a cheaper alternative in the DRM-602X, a double-speed drive which claims 307K/sec transfers and 300ms seek times, and costs about £600. Contact Pioneer free on 0800 480480.

CD-ROM formats and standards

There are a confusing number of different names around for various different CD-ROM formats and standards. Here's a quick look at what they're all about.

ISO 9660, High Sierra, Apple HFS, dual and split formats

The key one you need to know about is ISO 9660, which is the standard 'format' by which data on a CD-ROM disc is organised. It derives its name from its International Standards Organisation resolution number, but is also quite often called 'High Sierra', a name which derives from Del Webb's High Sierra Hotel and Casino at Lake Tahoe, Nevada, USA, where the group of boffins that defined this updated standard met for conferences.

All PC CD-ROMs use the ISO 9660 standard, as do Kodak Photo CD discs, which makes things nice and simple. Sony's MiniDisc system also uses ISO 9660 as its base, and with the appropriate software PCs that are equipped with a CD tray that can accommodate the smaller discs can also use MiniDisc software.

Discs for the Amiga CDTV and Amiga CD32, just in case you're curious, also use the ISO 9660 format, but of course the Amiga file-name standard is incompatible with PCs, never mind the fact that Amiga data can not be run on PC systems, or vice versa. All the same, it does mean that Amiga CD systems can read data such as text and picture files from PC ISO 9660 CD-ROMs, provided that they can translate them using appropriate conversion software.

The Apple Macintosh is a little bit different. Macs can read ISO 9660 quite happily, which leads to the widespread use of dual-format CD-ROM discs. Most Apple CD-ROMs, however, use the proprietary Apple HFS system, which is the same format used by Apple hard disk drives. The advantage of this is that HFS discs can use the full Apple Finder system to have proper Apple-style icons, whereas ISO 9660 discs on a Mac only have pseudo-icons with limited functionality.

Thanks to multi-session CD-ROM drives, it is quite possible to have a split-format CD-ROM with separate Macintosh and PC partitions, the advantage being that the Apple partition (or 'session') can use the full HFS system. This is the method that CD-ROM Today magazine uses for its cover discs.

Red book, yellow book, green book, white book

As already mentioned elsewhere, each of the various CD standards has been set out in a document and published as a handbook which all hardware and software makers can use to ensure that their equipment and discs are compatible with all other systems worldwide. Each is known as a book of a different colour.

The original was the Red Book, which describes CD Digital Audio. Next came the Yellow Book, which laid out the standard for CD-ROM and has since been modified to encompass CD-ROM XA and multi-session discs. This is still the most important for our purposes.

More recently, the Green Book has been published by Philips to set a standard for their CD-i player, which they still hope other manufacturers will adopt. Originally Sony and Matsushita were involved with CD-i, but they dropped out a long while back.

Most recent of the lot is the White Book, which covers the new Video CD system based around the MPEG1 standard for full-screen, full-motion video. Video CD is explained in full elsewhere in this book.

Showing off with two CD-ROM drives!

It's perfectly possible for you to fit more than one CD-ROM drive, and we hear that the latest piece of technological one-upmanship in the multimedia office is to work on a machine with two CD-ROM drives fitted – one is used exclusively to play audio CDs, while the other runs CD-ROM applications!

Chapter 4

Computer choices

- Computer types for beginners
- Computer terms for beginners
- Starting from scratch: PC or Mac?
- Other computers, and alternatives
- What's the future of CD-ROM?

This is a Philips CD-i player. Effectively it's a CD-ROM computer, but it's designed to look more like a video recorder so that it can sit comfortably in the living room, and it uses an infra-red remote control unit instead of a keybaord and mouse.

Introduction

In the previous chapter we looked at the ins and outs of CD-ROM formats and the CD-ROM drives themselves. But what about the rest of the computer system that goes along with the CD-ROM drive?

In the next chapter we'll go into specific details about PC-compatibles and the Apple Macintosh, which are the two most popular choices for a CD-ROM computer.

This chapter, however, is really aimed at people who don't already have a computer and perhaps aren't too confident about what the differences are between different makes and models. We'll explain a few of the most important technical terms, as well as looking at why the PC and Mac are the main choices – and what the alternatives are.

Why this book concentrates on PC and Mac

There are other choices of computer besides PC and Mac, as we'll see shortly. However, these two machines currently have the widest range of CD-ROM software available, if only because both are popular in the United States, where the development of CD-ROM software has been much more active in the crucial period of the last two or three years.

That's why we have concentrated on the Mac and PC when it comes to giving specific advice about choosing, buying and fitting hardware in the following chapters.

Computer types for beginners

Just in case you've never bought a computer before and you're not quite sure what you're up against, it's worth explaining what the differences between different makes and models of computer. If you know the difference between a PC and a Macintosh, please skip this bit.

Not everyone realises that there's a big difference between who makes a computer and what type of computer it is. A PC might be made by Wang, IBM, Hewlett Packard or Amstrad, and yet all these different makes will run the same software, because they're all PC-compatibles. On the other hand, if you buy a machine made by Apple, it will probably not be able to run that software. Different types of computer that cannot run the same software are referred to as different 'formats'.

It all comes down to the way the computer is made. Computers are defined by two things: the main silicon chip inside the computer, which is called the CPU (central processing unit) and the software which controls the CPU, which is called the operating system.

WHAT DOES IT MEAN?

Incompatible formats cannot run the same software either because they use a different CPU, or because they use a different operating system.

For instance, modern PC-compatibles use an Intel 286, 386 or 486 CPU, and software for them will not run on an Apple Macintosh, which uses a Motorola 68000-series CPU. On the other hand, the Commodore Amiga home computer uses the same 68000-series CPU as the Mac, but its has a completely different operating system, so software that runs on the Amiga will not run on the Mac.

In essence, this wouldn't be a terribly complicated concept (if it weren't for the PC-compatibles, which put a bit of a spanner in the works) because the general rule is 'different maker = different format'. Apple make the Macintosh, Commodore make the Amiga, Acorn make the Archimedes – and none of the three can run the others' software.

The trouble with the PC-compatibles is that lots and lots of different firms make them, and they can all run the same software. It all started when IBM made the original IBM PC. They decided that to ensure the PC's success as a business computer, they would declare it an 'open format' and allow any manufacturer to make machines which imitated their own. These are referred to as IBM PC-compatibles, or just PC-compatibles, or, more usually, simply as PCs.

So it boils down to this. You can buy a PC made by all kinds of different manufacturers, and you'll be able to run PC software, in just the same way that a VHS video will play VHS video tapes no matter who they're made by.

Alternatively, you can buy a Macintosh made by Apple, and you'll be able to run only Macintosh software. Or you can buy an Amiga, made by Commodore, and you'll be able to run only Amiga software. Or you can buy an Archimedes made by Acorn, and it will run only Archimedes software. These are the four most important formats currently in existence.

Computer specifications for beginners

Along with the make and model, there are four important figures that you will see quoted in any advertisement for a computer, and it's worth taking a moment to understand them. The four figures fall into two groups of two.

CPU type and clock speed

The first pair of figures covers the CPU type, and the speed at which the CPU runs. On an advertisement for a PC, for example, you might see the specification "33MHz 486DX", while a Macintosh might be described as having a "25MHz 68030". In each case, the first figure, expressed in MegaHertz, is the speed, and the second is the specific type of CPU chip.

As we've already seen, the CPU is the main chip inside the computer, and in actual fact, the CPU really is the computer itself. A program is essentially a list of instructions that tells the CPU what calculations to perform, and the calculations are all carried out inside the CPU.

Early PCs were built around a slightly different chip, the 8086, but modern PCs are based on Intel's range of CPUs identified by the numbers 286, 386 and 486. The latest is the 586 which, for reasons of their own, Intel decided to call the Pentium. Each new CPU is faster and better than the previous version.

Early Macs used the Motorola 68000 CPU but later models have used the newer 68030 or 68040. The new Power Macintosh uses a completely different Power PC chip developed by Intel in association with Apple and IBM.

Every CPU has a built-in clock, which controls how fast the CPU handles calculations. The speed of this clock is measured in MegaHertz, abbreviated to MHz, which means 'millions of cycles per second'.

So any computer's abilities are dictated by the type of CPU it has, and what the clock speed of the CPU is. Different variants of the same CPU might run at different speeds, so you'll see "25MHz 486SX" and "33MHz 486DX" variants mentioned in PC advertisements.

What's more, the clock speed is a relative measure, that applies only to one type of CPU, not an absolute one. So a 33MHz 486 PC will actually run more quickly than a 33MHz 386 machine.

An absolute measure of computer speeds does exist, but you'll only see it quoted very occasionally. It is MIPS, or Millions of Instructions Per

Second, which is a measure of how many millions of calculations the CPU can carry out every second.

RAM memory and hard disk drive memory

The second pair of figures covers two completely, utterly different things which are both referred to loosely as "memory", which can be very confusing if you're new to computers. These are RAM and hard disk drive capacity.

Hard disks, like floppy disks and CD-ROMs, are for storing computer data and so can be referred to as "memory", but it's best to refer to them as "storage" and use the term "memory" only for RAM.

On a CD-ROM the data is stored permanently and cannot be changed, which is why it's a 'read-only' medium. But on a floppy disk or a hard disk data is stored semi-permanently and can be changed, so these are 'read-write' media. The key thing about disk storage is that it retains the data when you switch off the computer, because the data is written onto the disk magnetically, in much the same way that music is stored on a cassette tape or video on a video tape.

In just the same way that cassette tapes are available as C60s or C90s, floppy disks are available in two sizes (double density and high density), but hard disk drives are available in a wide variety of storage capacities, measured in Megabytes and ranging from 20Mb right up to several thousand Mb.

TOP TIP

A common basic hard drive specification for Macs is 40Mb, but like most things in life you're better off with as much as possible and 80Mb is a better bet for a Mac, while 120Mb or 160Mb sizes are recommended for a multimedia PC.

Hard disk drives are used to store your programs and all the data belonging to the programs, as well as the operating system for the computer.

RAM is a completely different kettle of fish. The RAM, which stands (unhelpfully) for Random Access Memory, is a set of silicon chips inside the computer which can store data only as long as they are powered, and so lose all their data when you switch the computer off.

The RAM is the working area for the computer. When you run a program, the program is loaded from the hard disk drive into the RAM, and so is able to start sending its instructions to the CPU. All the data in a file associated with the program – a letter you are typing with a word processing program, for example – is also held in RAM, to as great an extent as possible. This is why, when you are working in a program, you should save your file to hard disk as often as possible, because if the computer crashes (computers occasionally get confused and 'freeze') and you have to switch it off, the data in the RAM will be lost.

As well as the programs that you are running, the RAM also has to hold the operating system of the computer – DOS or Windows on a PC, and Finder on the Mac – all the time the computer is working. Because of this, and because modern PCs and Macs can 'multi-task', running more than one program at the same time – and also because modern software that uses lots of colours takes up a lot of memory, too – the demand for RAM is enormous. The chips that make up RAM, though, are expensive, and so a compromise has to be reached.

TOP TIP

The basic specification for RAM memory on most Macs and PCs is 4Mb (again, RAM is measured in Megabytes), but to ensure that you can comfortably run all software, you would be well advised to opt for 8Mb when you are buying a new machine.

So to sum up, hard disk space (storage) and RAM (memory) are the two most important figures in a computer specification. When you are looking at advertisements, PC ads are usually pretty explicit – they'll say "4Mb RAM, 160Mb hard disk" – but Mac specifications slip these figures in next to the model name, such as "Quadra 8/160".

Which machine?

There's no doubt that the two most popular and active formats for CD-ROM are the Apple Macintosh and the PC-compatibles. If you're not committed to a particular type of computer, you're most likely to choose one of these two. But which?

The main thing that is likely to affect your choice will be whether you already have experience of either, and especially if you already use one of these at work. If you have a PC at work, it's useful to be able to run the same programs at home that you use at work, and the same thing applies if you are using a Mac at work. Not only can you bring work home, but also you already know how the computer works and are familiar with its quirks and its terminology.

But if you're making a completely fresh choice, there are a number of different factors that you'll have to weigh up.

PCs undoubtedly have a wider range of CD-ROM software available, and many of the PC CD-ROMs are better than their Mac equivalents. This is especially true of games, where the PC leads the way by a very wide margin, but even in the non-games arena, most of my favourite discs are for the PC. On the other hand, it's becoming increasingly common for the best discs to be released on both formats.

Good, modern PCs are also much more effective. A 33MHz 486 PC (we'll explain the jargon shortly, if you're unsure what '33MHz 486' means) generally runs CD-ROM software more quickly than the most powerful Macintosh, and it's really speed that makes all the difference. PCs are also much better at making economical use of memory, and so find it easy to run several programs at once.

The Mac does have its advantages, however. A Macintosh is altogether easier to set up and use, because it's been designed for simplicity. This ease of use makes a big difference. Using a Mac is generally a pleasure, whereas using a PC can often be a chore.

If you're buying a PC, you have to be prepared to get stuck in to some quite technical stuff – loading text files into an editing program and altering them to make sure everything runs properly, for example. It's not necessarily all that difficult, but it can be intimidating.

TOP TIP

To sum up, the best advice would be to try to get a look at the different kinds of CD-ROM discs you want to be able to use, and see whether the ones you want are on PC or Mac, and let that guide your choice. And if you decide on a PC, make sure you get it from somewhere where you can phone up and ask them to explain things you don't understand. 'Technical support', it's called.

Home computer alternatives to the Mac and PC

There are at least two other makes of computer that might make an alternative to the obvious choices of a PC or Mac. Their advantage is price, but in both cases the disadvantage is that the range of CD-ROM titles is far narrower than the PC or Mac.

Commodore Amiga 1200

Commodore might not be the best-known computer manufacturer in the world, but they actually created the world's first personal computer in the late 1970s. The Commodore 64, which was introduced in 1982 and stayed on sale for ten years in Britain, became the world's top-selling single model of computer. So the Amiga does come from a proven stable.

The Amiga range, based around the Motorola 68000 series of CPU chips (as used by the Apple Macintosh) was introduced in 1985 and by 1992 the Amiga A500 model had become Britain's best-selling home computer, with over a million machines in use in the UK alone. Its success was due mainly to its flexibility – a wide choice of excellent video games was available for it, but it could also perform well at word processing, DTP (DeskTop Publishing), music and video.

Commodore had long believed that CD-ROM would be the future of home computing, but their first attempt to break into this area of the market was the ill-fated CDTV, a non-computer 'concept machine' which rivalled the Philips CD-i. It did not succeed, and muddied the waters for Commodore's later attempt at creating a CD-ROM drive for the older A500 computer. This also failed to sell.

The A1200 is an entirely new model with a vastly updated specification, introduced in 1993. It costs only £299 and comes with 2Mb of RAM and a 32-bit 68020 CPU, as well as redesigned graphics chips that enable it to display 256 colours and so rival the standard used by PC-compatibles. The price includes neither a monitor (an extra £300 or so) nor a hard disk drive (£200 for one of a decent size), but it can be attached to an ordinary TV set and it can use miniature IDE drives fitted inside the compact case of the machine – the entire A1200 is little larger than its keyboard.

The A1200 was well received, but because it was a new design it could not take advantage of the enormous library of software that the older models of Amiga had built up.

Meanwhile, Commodore introduced another new version of the Amiga in the form of a 32-bit CD-based video games console, called the Amiga CD32. In late 1994, a third-party manufacturer introduced an add-on CD-ROM drive for the Amiga 1200 at a price of about £200. With this attached, the A1200 can run some of the old CDTV CD-ROM discs and most of the new games released for the CD32, but it has yet to see the release of any A1200-specific non-games titles, so it's not well served for education, reference and so on.

Added complications for the Amiga 1200 emerged when Commodore suffered a financial crisis. As this book goes into print, it is possible that the company might be salvaged (perhaps by a group of managers from the UK branch of Commodore, since the Amiga has been most successful in the UK) but the crisis has not been good for the Amiga's future.

Because the Amiga has lacked a stable commitment to non-games CD-ROM over the last three years, and because of the unstable financial situation, the Amiga 1200 cannot be recommended as a first choice for a new CD-ROM computer buyer.

For people who already own an Amiga 1200, however, the arrival of a proper CD-ROM drive for the machine could give it an additional lease on life which it would not otherwise have had. Even so, it seems unlikely to ever develop the range of software that the PC and Mac enjoy, if only because the Amiga now has no significant user base in the USA.

Acorn Archimedes

Acorn might never have made it into the big time were it not for an arrangement with the BBC (the British Broadcasting Corporation) by which the original 8-bit Acorn computer became the BBC computer in the early eighties.

It was a good machine, and the BBC's seal of approval gave it authority, but its future was assured when the computer was adopted by the Government as the standard model when the decision was made to equip all primary schools in Great Britain with the same make of computer.

That unassailable position at the heart of British education ensured the success of the machine, but it also stuck a label of 'educational' on all Acorn models which has since proved to be as much of a liability as an asset.

In the mid-eighties, when other manufacturers were moving towards the next generation of computing by releasing computers based around 16-bit CPUs to replace the older 8-bit models, Acorn decided that an appropriate follow-up to the BBC would be an extremely advanced machine that not only leapt ahead with a 32-bit design, but also was based around RISC (Reduced Instruction Set Computing) – a technique that makes programming much more efficient and so vastly increases the speed of operation of a computer. Apple have recently made much mileage out of the RISC techniques used in their Power Macintosh range, but Acorn were there well ahead of them.

The new machine was called the Archimedes, and originally was on sale at prices that made it equivalent to, and competitive with, the PC-compatibles. However, the Archimedes did not find a foothold in business use, and nor could it find a comfortable niche to settle into, the way the chic Apple Mac did with designers.

Its main foothold continued to be in education, where schools adopted it as a logical follow-up to the BBC, even though the Archimedes was a completely different type of computer. Acorn developed a strategy of reducing the price of the Archimedes to make it competitive in the home computer market which was becoming dominated by the Amiga, though the Archimedes remained the more expensive choice.

The current Archimedes models represent good value for money, particularly in the 'bundle' which is now widely available in high

As we go to press, Acorn' latest Risc PC600 with built in CD-ROM drive offers a worthy alternative to your standard multimedia Mac of PC. It uses a RISC (Reduced Instruction Set) processor, but for £99 you can add a card carrying a 486SX chip that effectively gives you dual processors. Although it has a 16-bit sound card already, for greater compatibility a Sound Blaster module is on the way, and also planned are Acorn video cards. It's early days yet, but Acorn could be about to have on offer a machine that will let you use all sorts of educational software, plus all the fun, games and powerful CD-ROM applications available for PCs.

street retailers, where the Archimedes A3000 model comes with a monitor and a printer for less than £1,000.

The Archimedes has also benefited from its educational connections when it comes to CD-ROM. Since CD-ROM software has massive potential use in education, Acorn had the incentive to develop a viable CD-ROM drive. Publishers of software who specialise in educational products have been quick to take advantage of this, and in fact a substantial proportion of the money provided by the UK Government to help the development of educational titles has gone to firms who publish Acorn titles, though very often these titles are also available for the PC.

What the Archimedes lacks, though, is support by entertainment publishers, so there is less of a choice of games. It is also a less obvious choice for general leisure interest, so the kind of reference and leisure titles that Microsoft publish are not so widely available for the Archie.

Which puts the Archimedes in third place as a choice of format, but it is still quite a long way behind the Mac or PC if you wish to get a machine for use in the home.

The Philips CD-i – a viable alternative?

There's an interesting alternative to traditional computers which can, in theory at least, open up very much the same interesting possibilities that CD-ROM computing does – and that's Philips's CD-i (Compact Disc Interactive) machine.

It looks more like a video recorder or a hi-fi component than a computer, and it's controlled using an infra-red remote control which features a small joystick and four buttons. Whatever it looks like, underneath the disguise it is essentially a computer containing a CD-ROM drive.

The CD-i is certainly a very good idea, and a concept whose time has almost come. The main problem is that when its time does come, the CD-i might be gazumped by a rival machine with a higher specification. The secondary problem is that the concept is rather a difficult one to explain to a mass audience, which is why Philips has had to spend an enormous amount of money on advertising in return for what's been to date a pretty humble result in actual sales.

Essentially, because it's a CD-ROM computer, the CD-i can play pretty decent video games – which is currently one of its main selling points – but can also be used for all sorts of other kinds of multimedia. So 'edutainment' titles for kids, such as an interactive episode of *Sesame Street*, and reference titles, like a tour of the Smithsonian museum, have featured heavily in Philips' publicity.

In theory, there is no reason why the CD-i shouldn't be just as good as the PC or Mac at running a typical CD-ROM application like an encyclopedia. Though to date, there aren't any CD-i titles to rival the best available on Mac and PC.

If one handicap for the CD-i is its lack of a keyboard, then that same thing turns into an advantage when you consider another capability of all CD-ROM systems – playing audio CDs. It might be nice to play

The Philips CD-i costs only £300 and yet can act as a hi-fi audio CD player and an in-the-living-room multimedia machine, with a wide range of games available (though fewer reference and edutainment discs). For £450, you can buy a version that includes all the hardware necessary to play Video CD discs.

music on your PC while you're working, but the PC is hardly a viable alternative to a hi-fi. Whereas a CD-i in the living room integrates completely into a hi-fi and TV system, and (potentially at least) puts all the educational, reference and leisure possibilities of CD-ROM into that living-room environment too.

The keystone in the CD-i concept is the addition of a Video CD cartridge (Video CD is explained in full elsewhere in this book). With this £150 add-on, the £299 CD-i becomes a Video CD player as well as audio CD player and 'home multimedia' player. That's quite a package.

The only real drawback for CD-i is that the concept is excellent, but the reality falls somewhat short. The specification of the CD-i as a computer was pretty impressive when it was being developed in the late eighties and early nineties, but is now looking a little aged and out-of-date. Its graphics resolutions and the number of colours it can display, and the speed at which it operates, are significantly inferior to modern PCs and Macs, never mind the dedicated CD-driven games consoles with which it will shortly be in competition.

This, together with the lack of applications of the quality of Microsoft's range for Windows PCs, will inevitably leave the CD-i looking second best compared with a computer if CD-ROM is your priority.

The long-term plan for Philips is to integrate CD-i increasingly with their hi-fi systems, so that you buy a midi system that includes tuner, amplifier, cassette player, and CD-i for audio CDs, Video CDs and home multimedia. As an idea, it could indeed work, but it would require a new, significantly improved version of the CD-i system to ensure its success.

CD-based video games consoles

If your primary interest in CD-ROM is in playing games, then there may be an exciting alternative to a PC in the form of one of the new generation of games consoles which are currently appearing on the market.

There is so much more to CD-ROM than games that it would seem to be a shame if that were your main priority, but at the same time, there's a great deal of evidence that a few outstanding CD-ROM games – particularly Virgin's *The 7th Guest* and LucasArts' Star Wars game *Rebel Assault* – were what prompted lots of PC owners to rush out and spend £150 on a CD-ROM drive.

On top of which, just because the main *raison d'etre* of these video games consoles is video games, that does not mean that they cannot be used for many other kinds of CD-ROM applications – encyclopedias, children's books, 'edutainment', 'infotainment' and all the rest.

Amiga CD32

This variant of the Amiga 1200 home computer takes the guts of the computer but replaces the keyboard and mouse with a 'joypad' controller, and the floppy and hard disk drives with a CD-ROM. It then sticks the whole lot in a compact grey case with a flip-up lid for the CDs to go into.

So the Amiga CD32 is a 32-bit video games console with 256 colours to play with, and according to developers it's a good one to work with. It's a pity that support for the CD32 is not very widespread among software publishers, because they don't see much of a market for the Amiga outside the UK, and not a large one even there.

So far, there are a number of pretty good games for the Amiga CD32, but they're all revamped versions of games previously released on floppy disk, the only concessions to the CD format being long intro animations and CD-quality soundtracks. The future for releases looks unspectacular, and for non-games titles, non-existent. The only other great advantage is that there's a Video CD cartridge available for the Amiga CD32 for an additional £200.

Sega Mega CD

Based on Sega's 16-bit, 256-colour Megadrive games console of *Sonic the Hedgehog* fame, the popularity of which was huge between 1990 and 1993, the Mega CD has been responsible for a healthy share of CD-based games sales to date.

Its up-take on release in 1993 was pretty healthy because at the time all the pundits were talking about CDs being the future for games, which gave it enough of a user base for it to figure pretty prominently in the software sales charts. At the time, though, it was a slightly bigger fish than the others but only in a very small pond, and sales of the machine are waning very rapidly as the game-players in its teenage target audience eagerly anticipate the arrival of a new generation of games consoles, including a new machine from Sega themselves.

Since the Mega CD is significantly more expensive than its cartridge-based brother, and since it has no real future in video games, never mind any other form of multimedia, it's not a real prospect.

Panasonic 3D0 and the next generation

When the news of it first broke in late 1992, the 3D0 sounded like a world-beater. Trip Hawkins, charismatic leader of entertainment software creators Electronic Arts, had overseen the secret development of a 32-bit video games console driven by CD, which featured specialised graphics chips that would help it manipulate 3D graphics at a speed previously unheard of, heralding the arrival of an amazing new generation of video games.

What happened next was intriguing. With the prototypes still not fully functional, Hawkins floated the 3D0 Company on the US stock exchange and announced that they would not make the 3D0 machine. Instead, licences to manufacture it would be sold to leading electronics firms across the world. If the plan succeeded, 3D0 could become a standard format for CD-based video games.

Panasonic were the first to sign up to make 3D0 machines and the first to market them, though others, such as Sanyo, are also working on their own versions. Like video recorders or CD players, the 3D0 made by different firms will look different, but will all run the same software.

The 3D0 caused a great deal of excitement among pundits and its future looked assured. But before it could go on sale, the 3D0 needed a substantial amount of decent software to be available, and so a lull followed. Eventually, 3D0 appeared in limited numbers in America

The Panasonic 3DO offers some great new games titles like Road Rash and Fifa International Soccer. It heralds the new generation of games consoles, but no longer promises to set a universal standard.

shortly before Christmas 1993, and finally arrived in the UK in autumn 1994.

The trouble that 3D0 now faces is that the critical environment that was so favourable for it in 1992 has changed a great deal subsequently. Previously, the specification of the machine seemed thoroughly impressive, but now that Atari's 64-bit Jaguar is on sale and Sega, Nintendo and Sony all have new wonder-machines in the pipeline for 1995 it looks less of a good bet.

There is an undercurrent of feeling within the video games industry that it would be a good thing if one particular format were to become a standard, so that the energy of programmers and developers would not have to be wasted converting games to run on many different types of machine. One benefit of 3D0 was that it seemed poised to become a standard because of the licensing system, but since its specification is now seen as inferior, 3D0 now seems a less desirable standard to have.

So the question now is 'what happens instead?' Currently, everyone's playing a waiting game. There's a quiet spell in the sales of video games consoles, with the 'last generation' of popular machines, the 16-bit, cartridge-driven Sega MegaDrive and Nintendo Super NES, showing a steep decline in sales. At the same time there's also a quiet spell in development, with games for the Mega CD and PC CD-ROM filling the vacuum to a certain extent.

This is part of the reason why PC CD-ROM is enjoying a period of – comparatively – immense success. Buyers who might otherwise have been attracted by a video games console are spending substantially more money on PCs because it's where the most exciting games are happening, because it's more future-proof, and because the PC can do lots of other things besides run games.

This temporary calm is nearing its end, however, since games publishers now have development equipment with which they can work on programming games for at least two of the next-generation systems – Sega's Saturn and Sony's PSX or Playstation, both due for release in 1995. Nintendo's Project Reality, which is said to incorporate the technology used by Silicon Graphics workstations, remains more of a mystery.

The single, common format being something of a Holy Grail for video games publishers, the critics have spent a great deal of effort trying to analyse which of the new 'next generation' consoles is Most Likely to Succeed. There's an assumption that whichever is the strongest, not just in terms of specification but also in terms of the marketing muscle of its manufacturer, will win out and become the world standard. And the one that's getting the vote of forward-looking technology critics like Future Publishing's own *Edge* magazine is the Sony PSX.

We've been down this road many times before, however, and never before has one single system become a de facto standard, whatever its merits over its rivals. It seems equally unlikely to happen this time around, especially when the rivals are Sega, Nintendo and Sony, none of whom will submit easily.

By 1996, then, you could have a choice of three new CD-driven consoles – the Sony, Sega and 3D0 – with the Atari Jaguar also expected to have an add-on CD drive. Only Nintendo are determined to stick to the ROM-chip-based cartridge.

All these machines will be designed principally for video games, but will also be able to play audio CDs. And all of them could be available in versions that play Video CD discs. Moreover, any one of them will also be capable of running excellent multimedia discs of the non-games kind – reference, children's, 'edutainment', 'infotainment' and all the rest – provided only that they sell in sufficient numbers, or the manufacturers are dedicated enough to that area of the market for someone to develop the titles.

Which means that any one of them could slot equally well into the home multimedia, CD-entertainment slot that Philips CD-i has mapped out. This market for multi-faceted machines could become the most important one as it slowly gains public acceptance, and any of these machines could succeed equally well. It's a wide-open race.

The future of CD entertainment?

Since we're already peering into the crystal ball to some extent with our look at the future of video games consoles, we might as well take a deeper look and consider some of the other possibilities for a living-room multimedia machine in years to come.

Jumping on the bandwagon, we're talking Information Superhighway here. The theory is that cables into the home could bring us a much greater choice of television, to the extent that we can not only decide what we watch but also 'interact' with the programmes, and this could also bring us access to immense libraries of information and multimedia software.

If this happens, there are two different 'models' for how it might happen. Either the processing power that gives us the choices could be centrally located and accessed remotely via the cables, or we could have 'set-top boxes' which are analogous to a satellite TV tuner, but more like a personal computer, with which we can filter and access whatever data we want from the networks.

In this latter scenario, a simple idea like Philips CD-i becomes the precursor for the complete entertainment system of the future. The

CD-i is a flexible, adaptable, programmable system that's entirely different from the dumb, linear action of a CD player or a video recorder.

In a way, though, the video recorder is the ideal model of what the future might look like. With a TV and a video, you can either watch what's currently being broadcast, or you can 'download software', by recording a programme to watch it later – or you can pop out and buy pre-recorded software by getting a video cassette.

Similarly, a CD-based multimedia system could have the same relationship with the information superhighway that the video currently has with the broadcast network. You could use interactive TV or multimedia software in real time, over the network. You could download it, for use at any time, or you could pop out and buy audio, video or interactive CDs to keep and re-use as often as you wish.

That's all in the future, and this future could develop in any number of different ways. What is currently evident, though, is the convergence of technologies that makes it possible. And it's not just in primitive form in the CD-i, either.

Apple have just released a Macintosh that incorporates a TV tuner, so that with a CD-ROM drive and a Video CD card you can watch TV, play CD music, watch CD videos, or do computery things like word processing, all on the same machine. IBM have developed a version of the Power PC chip specifically for use in set-top boxes, and an American firm has already released a CD-driven, Windows-based set-top style box that mirrors a CD-i, but does it with standard PC technology.

The possibilities are far more numerous than the certainties, But one thing is for sure – with all this convergence of technology, it's a good time to be investing in a CD-ROM computer, because that's where all the new developments are happening first. A CD-ROM system is a step into the future.

Chapter 5
CD-ROM hardware

- Is my current machine good enough?
- Minimum specs for Macs and PCs
- The MPC standard explained
- Choosing a new Mac or PC
- Multimedia upgrade kits explained

A typical multimedia upgrade kit should include a CD-ROM drive, stereo speakers, a 16-bit sound card, some headphones and a speaker, and some CD-ROM software to get you started.

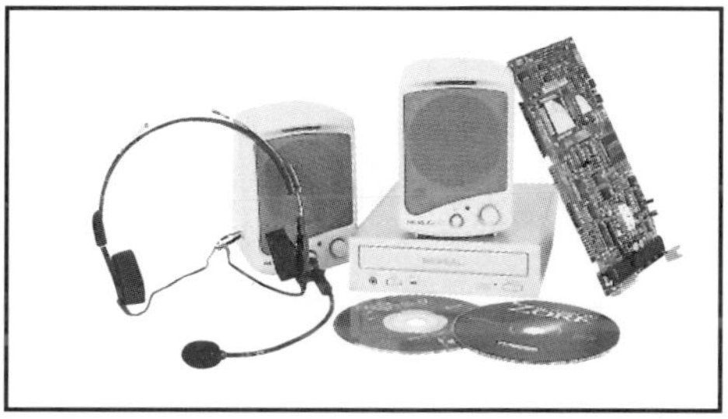

Introduction

Assuming that an Apple Macintosh or some make of PC is the best bet for CD-ROM, what do you need to know before you can get up and running?

Well, first of all you might already have a computer: so is it good enough to run the latest CD-ROM software? And if not, what do you need to do to it to get it ready? And on the other hand, if you don't already have a Mac or PC, what should you look for when you're shopping around for a good deal?

By the end of this chapter you should know exactly what you need to buy to get yourself a state-of-the-art CD-ROM system. We'll start with the minimum specifications which your machine will need to reach.

Setting minimum specifications for CD-ROM

Whether it's a Mac or PC you've decided on and whether you're upgrading an existing machine by adding a CD-ROM drive or starting completely from scratch, there are certain minimum standards that your machine will have to reach.

In every case, the requirements of the hardware are defined by the needs of the software. Good, exciting, modern CD-ROM software makes extensive use of video clips, full-colour pictures and high-quality sound, and all of these things are very demanding on a computer.

Computer speed doesn't mean CD-ROM speed

The processing power of a computer is always measured by the speed of the processor: a PC or Mac with a faster processor will tend to run programs more quickly. What you might think are quite trivial amounts of time – seconds, or even fractions of a second – do become very noticeable when it's time that you're spending looking at a blank screen while the computer works out what you told it to do.

So in general terms, processing speed is the key factor when buying a computer, and of course the faster the computer you buy, the more expensive it will be. But there is one important thing to bear in mind, and that's the fact that processing speed does not necessarily speed up the rate at which CD-ROM applications run.

That's because CD-ROM drives are handicapped by the speed at which they can read data from a CD-ROM disc and pass it to the RAM of the computer. Even a double-speed CD-ROM drive, transferring data at 300K/sec or faster, is incredibly slow compared to the rate at which a hard drive can pass data to the computer.

For this reason, processing speed need not be your only consideration if you are buying a computer especially for CD-ROM. You can opt for a cheaper, slower machine, and you won't necessarily notice the difference.

The operation of all CD-ROM discs is, however, controlled by an 'executable', a program which runs in the RAM of the computer and controls which data is read from the CD-ROM disc at any particular moment. These programs are often transferred to your computer's hard disk drive so that they are more quickly accessible, and will in any case run more quickly and efficiently on a computer with a faster processor. So while processing speed is not a key factor, it does still make a difference.

Macintosh CD-ROM: where to start

What sort of a basic machine do you need for Macintosh CD-ROM? Well, the older Mac Plus, SE or Classic models with the small, built-in screen are right out. The deciding factor for Mac owners is the screen display. While some older CD-ROM discs work with a ten-inch Classic screen, by far the majority require a minimum of a 13-inch colour monitor.

Other things you'll generally need are System 7, 4Mb of RAM and the speed given by a 68020 or faster processor, so the minimum system requirement is usually taken as the now-discontinued LCII model.

Components of a Mac CD-ROM system

Compared with a PC, where interfaces, sound cards and the like complicate the issue enormously, the Mac CD-ROM system is incredibly simple. This is all you need…

- **The Macintosh itself**
- **CD-ROM drive, fitted internally or plugged in externally**
- **Powered amplifying stereo speakers (optional)**

Minimum specification for Macintosh CD-ROM

Here's a more detailed run-through of the sort of hardware specification you'll need in a Mac CD-ROM system. Unlike the MPC standard for PCs, there is no set minimum for the Mac, so our recommendations are based our experience of the sort of hardware Mac CD-ROM discs expect you to have. We'll summarise the figures later for your quick reference.

Hard drive

You don't have to have an enormous hard drive. If you don't do lots of high-end graphics, video or DTP work yourself (all of which create enormous files), and you don't have dozens of programs you want to store, and you're willing to delete old stuff rather than hanging on to everything, then you could comfortably get away with the bare minimum of 40Mb. If you want a little more elbow room go for 80Mb, but only if your non-CD-ROM needs are pretty demanding would you need a 120Mb hard drive or higher.

Having said that, extra hard drive space does give you the luxury of being able to leave the control programs for CD-ROM applications sitting around on your hard drive (see 'Installing CD-ROM software', below). For laziness' sake alone, then, 120Mb would be a good first bet, but if your money is tight don't feel forced to go for a more expensive model with a larger hard drive.

Throw in some powered speakers, and this would be your multimedia Macintosh set-up. This one's got a built in CD-ROM drive, and notice the deep Quadra housing it's got. That means plenty of room for extra hardware goodies like video cards.

RAM

System 7 uses an enormous amount of memory before you even start running any other applications, which ups the memory requirements of the Mac quite hugely. In theory there is no good reason why 4Mb shouldn't be fine (and you can get by with it quite happily), but to be perfectly practical you really should double that to at least 8Mb. Only a few Mac CD-ROM discs specifically require 8Mb, but most of them will behave much better with 8Mb.

Video RAM

You'll need a Mac that can power a 256-colour 13-inch screen (though the standard monitor nowadays is a 14-inch), so the minimum is a Mac LCII. As standard, Macs come with the capability to use 256 colours on the screen at one time, and so that's the standard minimum requirement which CD-ROM applications look for: but Macs can also be expanded to use more colours if you fit extra video RAM.

The Mac, with its pleasant tendency to state things simply, describes the different colour options over 256 colours as 'thousands' and 'millions'. The 'thousands' option represents 16-bit colour which gives about 65,000 colours on the screen, whereas the 'millions' option is shorthand for full 24-bit photographic-quality colour, with over 16 million colours available.

All Mac CD-ROMs have 256-colour displays, but some will use an enhanced 24-bit display if you have the capacity. The 'thousands of colours' option is very seldom used. So few CD-ROMs use 24-bit colour that this should not be a factor that affects your decision – the only reason you're likely to adopt 24-bit colour is if your non-CD uses of the Mac require it, perhaps for graphics or DTP work. One great advantage of 24-bit colour, though, is the ability to view Kodak Photo CD images in true photographic colour.

Box size

Only the bottom-of-the-range LC475 now comes in the smaller case, but if you already own an LC model, this may be a factor in wanting to upgrade. The only real difference between the LCs and larger Macs like the Centris and Quadra is the larger cases of the latter, which means they have space inside for several expansion cards, whereas the LC has room for only one half-size card.

Generally, most people don't want or need to add expansion cards to their Macs, but you might wish to buy a Video CD (MPEG1) card like the RealMagic, which would leave you with no space for anything else, such as a network card or video card.

Double-speed CD-ROM drive

Just as you can get by with 4Mb of RAM, you can also get by with a single-speed CD-ROM drive, which are now very cheap. But any modern CD-ROM application will run at a painfully slow crawl, and QuickTime video clips will barely run at all. Don't compromise: go for double-speed.

System Extensions

There are a number of System Extensions required to power your CD-ROM drive, but these will be provided on a floppy disk along with your drive. There are also a couple of others that are frequently used by CD-ROM applications, especially QuickTime and Sound Manager: but any disc that uses these will have copies of them on the CD, so that you can install them into the System folder on your hard disk drive before you run the disc. So Extensions aren't something you have to worry about either.

Powered speakers

Entirely optional, these, because you don't actually need them in order to be able to run CD software. However, the speaker inside the Mac is a little bit small and tinny, and it's also mono, so for the full benefit of the sounds and music on CD-ROM discs – especially when you consider that many CD-ROMs are mixed-mode discs that have full hi-fi quality CD-DA audio – it's well worth getting a set of powered speakers. Turn the volume up, and even the tone the Mac makes on start-up becomes an impressive orchestral harmony!

The powered speakers are just like Walkman speakers, and indeed it can be a good bargain to get a set of powered headphones instead of the specifically computer-orientated versions you see on sale. The powered speakers plug into the stereo mini-jack connector on the back of the Mac, and an amplifier in the speakers boosts the sound level and quality. Remember that you can also plug headphones into the same jack socket. The speakers are normally powered from the mains, but some are powered from batteries, which is a less economical option.

Two other things are worth mentioning. The audio supplied to the speakers is a mixed signal that combines both pure CD-DA audio and also computer-generated sounds, the latter including soundtracks to videos, for example, which derive from CD-ROM XA Mode 2 interleaved audio. An external CD-ROM drive such as the AppleCD 300 also has a jack and a volume control on the front into which you can plug speakers or headphones, but this will supply only CD-DA audio.

The other thing is that all Apple CD-ROM drives come with a program called CD Remote which can be used for playing audio CDs on the CD-ROM drive, which makes it even more worthwhile having powered speakers. And CD Remote will happily run in the background while you use normal hard-disk-based software on your Macintosh: music while you work!

Summary of minimum specification for Mac CD-ROM

- **Macintosh LCII or better, with 68020, 68030 or 68040 CPU and capable of powering 256-colour, 13-inch monitor or above**
- **System 7**
- **4Mb of RAM but preferably 8Mb RAM**
- **40Mb hard drive**
- **Double-speed CD-ROM drive**
- **Optional powered stereo speakers**

Choosing a Macintosh model

Choosing a brand new Mac would be simplicity itself (since the range is so small and all the models in the current range are more than capable of meeting the minimum specification for Mac CD-ROM), if it weren't for the slight complication of the new Power Macintosh models. We'll leave that aside for just a moment, though, and first take a look at a couple of other factors that might influence your decision.

The bottom-of-the-range Mac nowadays is the LC475. Bottom-of-the-range it may be, but when you consider that it's as powerful as the top-of-the-range Mac was two years ago, and yet costs about a quarter of the price, it's an excellent deal. The basic specification model costs about £1,000 including monitor, which is superb value for money.

However, the LC475 is the only Mac model that now comes in a slimline case, so you can't buy it with a built-in CD-ROM drive – you'll have to opt for an external drive instead.

One other important factor that may influence your decision is that both larger machines in the range, the Centris and Quadra, are available as AV models.

TOP TIP

The AV Macs incorporate hardware and software that enables you to digitise sound and video, and so if at any stage you are planning to create your own multimedia presentations, and AV Mac would be a good investment.

Prices of Macs are set by individual dealers, and you can find out who your local suppliers are by telephoning Apple (dial 100 for the operator and ask for Freefone Apple). All new Macs come with a one-year on-site repair warranty.

The Power Macintosh

The slight complication with the new Power Mac range, introduced by Apple in the spring of 1994, is that they are not actually Macs at all. They are a completely different format of computer.

The Power Mac is based around the Power PC 601 CPU chip, the first of a new range of processors developed in a cooperative venture between IBM, Apple and Intel. IBM and other PC manufacturers will also be building computers around the same chip, so to that extent the Power Mac is the herald of the ending of the divisions between the Mac and PC platforms.

In theory, the Power PC chip makes the Power Mac vastly more powerful than existing Macs. It uses RISC (Reduced Instruction Set Computing) techniques which, by cutting down the number of instructions needed to write a program, actually makes programs run much more quickly. It is also clocked at 60, 66 or 80 MHz in the various models in the Power Mac range.

Powered up: the Power Macintosh is big and powerful, but awaits native multimedia software. It does, however, run normal Mac software, only it's a bit slower and problems are not unheard of.

However, there's an awful lot more to the story than that. The Power PC chip incorporates full emulation of the Motorola 68040 chip, the latest of the family of chips used in all the pre-Power Mac models of Macintosh. Basically, there's an area on the chip which looks and behaves more or less exactly like a 68040. The Power Mac places the Power PC chip into the hardware of a Mac and uses an updated version of the Mac's Finder operating system to run it. Therefore, treating the Power PC chip as a 68040, it ought to be able to run all existing Mac software.

The truth is that it nearly does, but not quite, because the Power PC chip is not a true 68040 and so the program code has to be messed about with a bit by the new parts of the system before it reaches the 68040 emulator. For example, the Authorware program which *CD-ROM Today* magazine uses to compile its cover disc presentations would not originally work on the Power Mac, though the program was quickly updated and now works fine.

An even more surprising fact is that if you buy a Power Mac, it will most likely run your existing Mac software, but in spite of the extra speed and power of the Power PC chip, and the extra money you've paid, the Mac software will not necessarily run as quickly or efficiently as it does on an old-fashioned, 68040-based Mac. You get no extra 'bangs' for the extra bucks, as they say in the States.

Another supposed benefit of the Power Mac is that it will run Windows software, which again is not quite true. Most, but not all, Power Macs come with a software emulator for Windows which will run certain Windows programs as quickly as most PCs do. But it will not run any software that uses Windows Enhanced mode, which includes most of the worthwhile Windows software and nearly all Windows CD-ROM titles.

The true power of the Power Mac will only become apparent with the release of new, specially-programmed software that works directly with the Power PC chip, not at the 68040 emulator part of it. Lots of this new software, known as 'native' software, is on the way and will no doubt be blindingly impressive – but remember, it's not Mac software as we know it today.

As for the future... well, in a couple of years' time Apple will probably no longer be making or selling traditional 68040-based Macs at all, but at least you will be able to take all your hardware and software with you when you upgrade to a Power Mac.

Inevitably many people will be reluctant to change, but after all, the Power Mac still has Apple's ultra-friendly user interface, which is the main reason for using a Mac. And native Power Mac applications will be so much better than current Mac software that you'll be forced to change in order to get the latest and best versions of classic Mac applications like Adobe *PhotoShop* and *QuarkXPress*.

Multimedia upgrade kits for the Mac

Because there isn't the same need for a sound card or interface card to be fitted inside the Mac, all-in-one multimedia upgrade packages are

An Apple multimedia upgrade kit: no need to worry about a sound card or internal interface, this is the meaning of plug-and-play.

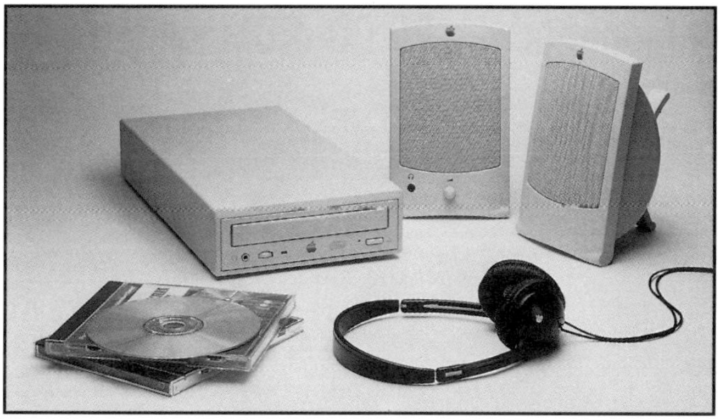

less common for the Mac and really only involve a CD-ROM drive plus stereo speakers and some free CD-ROM discs.

When you buy an Apple CD-ROM drive, you usually get some example discs free with it anyway, and you may be able to choose which discs you get, which can mean you can get your CD-ROM collection off to a good start without spending extra money.

PC CD-ROM: where to start

Essentially, the minimum machine you're going to need as a basis from which to start will be a 386 PC. Older 286 models are capable of powering a CD-ROM drive and running many of the simplest applications, but for modern Windows CDs with a heavy emphasis on graphics and video, you need more processing power than a 286 can offer.

It doesn't need to be a flashy, fast 486 PC that you start from, however: if you have a 386SX running at 25MHz, you should be OK, though inevitably the superior performance of a faster 486 machine will bring better all-round results from all kinds of software, not just CD-ROM applications.

Components of a PC CD-ROM system

A PC CD-ROM machine – very often called simply a "multimedia PC" – is slightly more complex than a Macintosh system, for several reasons.

To get the full benefit of most CD-ROM applications you will need to fit a sound card inside your PC. And because the PC does not have a standard SCSI interface, like the Mac, you'll need an interface card of some kind, which also fits inside the PC, to control the CD-ROM drive. Fortunately, many sound cards also act as CD-ROM drive interfaces.

For the quality of graphics used in CD-ROM applications, you will also need a video card that can provide SVGA graphics, and a compatible monitor to display those graphics. Also, you'll need a mouse, which may mean another interface card.

- **The PC itself, comprising motherboard, hard disk drive, floppy disk drive, RAM and keyboard**
- **Video card and SVGA monitor**
- **Microsoft-compatible mouse. Many CD-ROM applications are mouse-controlled.**
- **Not only DOS but also Windows operating system**
- **Double-speed CD-ROM drive**
- **CD-ROM drive interface, or SCSI interface (but this can be provided by the sound card)**
- **Sound card**
- **Optional stereo powered speakers**

Minimum specification for PC CD-ROM

In a moment, we'll run through a more detailed description of the kind of specification you ought to be looking for in a good multimedia PC. But first, a word about the MPC standard.

When you're choosing a multimedia PC, the MPC standard really ought to help you out. MPC stands for Multimedia PC, simply enough, and it is a standard defined by an organisation called the Multimedia PC Marketing Council. This body was set up by hardware manufacturers and software publishers to define a standard minimum PC specification that the hardware makers could stick to, and which gave the software writers a definite idea of what sort of system their software could aim at. This would mean, also, that the consumer could buy a machine with an MPC logo and know that it would run all software that carried the MPC logo.

There are several slight drawbacks. One is that the MPC standard was originally set a couple of years ago and quickly came to seem too low. So it was replaced by a second standard, known unsurprisingly as MPC2, which many PC experts agree is actually too high – you don't need a machine of MPC2 quality in order to be able to run comfortably all the PC CD-ROM titles currently on sale.

The other slight problem is that manufacturers have to pay a subscription to the organisation before they can use the MPC logo, so not all of them bother. This doesn't mean that their software or hardware is not up to the MPC standard, though.

Instead of the MPC logo, many software publishers print a complete listing of the minimum PC hardware specification required to run the software. For this reason alone, you ought to become familiar with the specification of your PC set-up, so that you can compare it with the requirements on a software box.

As we've already said, the MPC2 requirements are actually a little more than you really need, so in the following section we've described what we believe is the minimum specification, and there's a summary of that at the end of the section. But we've also printed both the MPC1 and MPC2 standards, for reference.

Processor and speed

The type of PC you buy is defined by the type of processor inside it – 386, 486 and so on. The Intel series of processors which PCs are built around have developed over the years, and every so often Intel have released a new chip giving it a new number in the series.

But there are also different versions of the same chip, capable of running at different speeds and these are defined by an extra couple of letters in addition to the chip number – hence 486SX and 486DX.

The older 386SX and 386DX machines are perfectly capable of running almost all Windows and CD-ROM software, but the newer 486SX models give a noticeable increase in performance in exchange for a fairly small increase in price, and so 486SX machines are currently the favourite with PC buyers.

A 486DX chip is pretty similar to the 486SX, but it includes a built-in maths co-processor (extra circuitry that handles mathematical calculations), which means it runs faster. 486DX chips will often run at speeds up to 50MHz, but these faster versions need the rest of the PC's motherboard (the main circuitry that surrounds the processor chip) to be made to an equally high standard, and so can be expensive.

TOP TIP

A cheaper way of getting a faster machine is to buy one with a 486DX2 chip installed. The DX2 is what's known as a 'clock doubled' chip and will normally run a 66MHz, but only requires the motherboard to be able to

operate at the normal 33MHz, making it cheaper to manufacture and therefore cheaper to buy.

A pretty recent arrival is the Pentium chip, which is what Intel have decided to call the processor that follows the 486 in the series and so would otherwise have been called the 586. The reaction to the Pentium amongst critics was not too warm, the general judgement being that it did not give a significant advantage for the extra price. Pentium chips proved difficult to manufacture, and so their specification in early releases had to be limited.

A more warmly-received release was Intel's DX4 processor, which is similar to a DX2 except faster – 'clock tripled' – and shares the DX2's advantage of using an existing 32-bit motherboard.

TOP TIP

However, all these mega-fast processors are far more than you really need. In practice, a 25MHz 486SX or a 33MHz 486DX will be more than adequate to run the best CD-ROM software.

One last feature to watch out for is 'Local Bus'. The bus is the main channel that all data travels through on its way to or from the CPU. The long-established ISA (Industry Standard Architecture) restricts that flow to 8 bits at a time flowing at a speed of just 8MHz, even on 16-bit PCs with much faster processors. Local Bus motherboards allows 32-bit transfer at speeds of 33MHz.

It sounds good, and it is. But the drawback is that it will only give you any extra performance if your graphics card and hard disk controller card also use a Local Bus system. Local Bus motherboards without Local Bus cards give you no advantage at all.

A typical multimedia PC system doesn't look all that different from a normal PC except that it has speakers and the CD-ROM drive in the front. Hidden inside the case are the three vital components: CD-ROM drive, sound card and a good video card.

Hard disk drives

Windows software is pretty demanding of hard disk space, and it's not uncommon for a single, simple program such as a word processor to take up as much as 20Mb of hard disk space. For that reason, you need a machine with a great deal of hard disk space, though not as much as some people would like you to believe. Fortunately, too, hard disk drives are now an awful lot cheaper than they were a couple of years ago, and for the same money you would then have paid for a 40Mb hard drive, you can now get one with four times the capacity.

TOP TIP

If you are buying a new machine, we would recommend that you look for one with at least a 120Mb or 170Mb hard drive.

RAM

Again, it's the demands of Windows that have caused a great increase in the specifications and needs of modern PCs. Most DOS programs work fine within the 640K limits of a PC's base memory, but Windows requires a good deal more besides.

It is just about possible to run Windows on a machine with only 2Mb of RAM, but there is one serious drawback. When it doesn"t have sufficient space in RAM to handle all the data it needs at one time, Windows will read and write data to the hard disk drive – it's called using 'virtual memory' – which slows operations down immensely. This is the principal cause of poor performance in Windows PCs.

For this reason, when you are buying a multimedia PC you should opt for at least 4Mb of RAM, which is the minimum sensible requirement. You will find it more convenient if you go for 8Mb of RAM, even though the vast majority of Windows software does not need this much.

You'll only need as much as 16Mb of RAM if you are going to do a lot of work with graphics software, perhaps if you are considering creating your own multimedia presentations.

Graphics card

Windows often needs complex graphical displays which, because they are at a high resolution and use a large number of colours, contain a lot of data. What's more, these graphics displays need to be updated on the screen at a very high rate.

As a result, many older VGA (Video Graphics Array) cards can't keep up, and slow the whole machine down. Currently, the in-vogue solution is a Super VGA Windows accelerated graphics card, which is rapidly becoming a standard piece of equipment on all PCs. It contains its own processors which handle calculations for the screen display, as well as its own RAM to hold data (usually 1Mb), thereby giving a vast increase in speed which can be used to make much more colourful, higher-resolution screen displays a reality.

Even many entry-level PCs now have an S-VGA card and so can display very high resolutions (640 pixels by 480 pixels and 800 by 600 are the most commonly used) as well as giving the ability to use up to 16 million colours on the screen in full 24-bit colour. An S-VGA card is an absolute necessity for a multimedia PC.

Why a separate card, though? Well, some PCs do have built-in graphics capability, but the advantage of a separate card fitted in an expansion slot inside the PC's case is that it gives you the freedom to uprate your PC's graphics in the future without having to change the whole machine.

Monitors

Most PCs come with 14-inch Super-VGA screens as standard (the monitor must be S-VGA so that it can handle the output from the S-VGA graphics card), and such a monitor will do fine. But there are a couple of points which are worth bearing in mind.

For starters, what does that 14-inch measurement represent? Well, unlike most TVs, only one measurement is quoted for a monitor, and that's the diagonal measurement of the tube itself. The area of the tube that you can actually see once a case has been fitted around it can vary considerably, so not all 14-inch monitors are equal: they don't all have the same size of visible display.

Something that's well worth looking out for on a monitor is the addition of height and width controls which allow you to adjust the area of the screen that you can see, and this is especially true if you are using Windows. For starters, you will be using lots of different graphics resolutions and so you need to adjust the size and shape of your picture. It's also an advantage to be able to adjust the horizontal and vertical positioning of the image on the screen. With the standard VGA resolution of 640 by 480 pixels, you can't spread lots of small windows all over the screen and flick from one to the other. By the time you're using S-VGA, however, with an 800 by 600 pixels display, you can put lots of little windows all round the screen, but some of the text will be too small to read. An ideal solution is to be able to see into the corners of the picture using the controls on your monitor.

You might wish to have a larger monitor, but when you're sitting in front of it for lengthy periods, a larger size such as a 17-inch display can get to seem oppressively big. An ideal compromise, significantly and comfortably larger but not so big as to be overwhelming, is a 15-inch size, and 15-inch monitors also often come with an FST (flatter, squarer tube) which gives a truer picture.

Mouse

Almost all PCs nowadays come with Windows, and therefore have a Microsoft-compatible mouse along with the connections for it and the software drivers it needs. If your PC doesn't already have a mouse then it very likely isn't a modern 386 or better, and so you'll probably be looking at getting a completely new PC anyway.

DOS and Windows

MS-DOS versions 5 or 6 are pretty handy, with version 6 the favourite because of its improved memory handling. Windows version 3 or better is vital – although there are a lot of CD-ROM applications that run from DOS, especially games, the vast majority of the best non-games stuff runs from Windows.

Double-speed CD-ROM drive

TOP TIP

We've said it before, but it's worth reiterating that you should not opt for a single-speed CD-ROM drive, no matter how cheap it is. Single-speed

Windows is an absolute necessity on any modern PC, CD-ROM or no, and version 3.1 is probably the minimum requirement for CD-ROM. The new Windows '95 version, which means you can go without DOS, will be mch quicker and more effective.

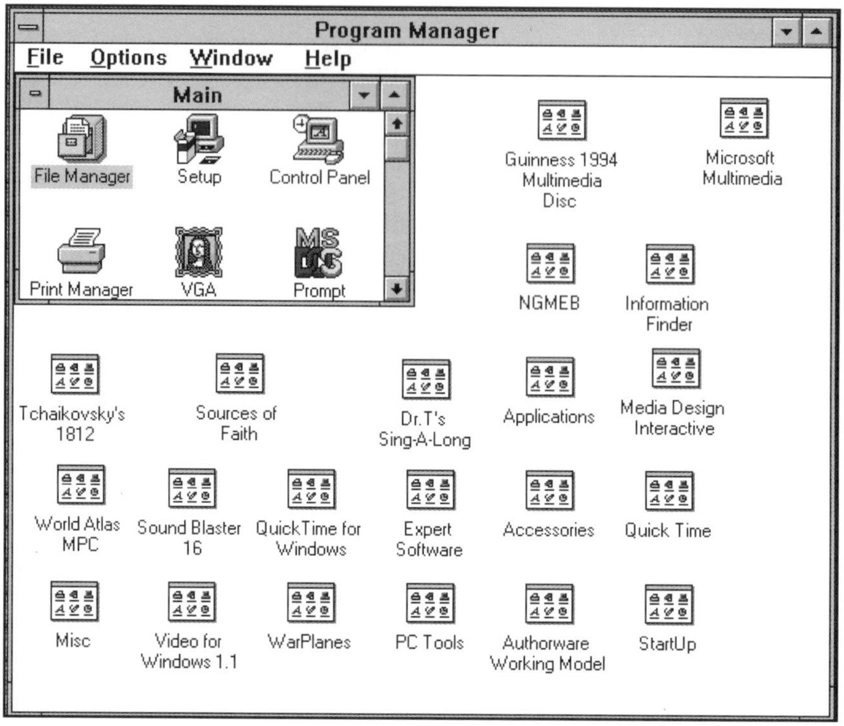

drives are not capable of handling the video clips that are a highlight of many CD-ROM titles.

Most likely, your CD-ROM drive will be fitted inside the case of your PC. External add-on CD-ROM drives are available if you're upgrading your existing machine, but you're going to have to take the lid off to fit a sound card or interface card anyway, so you might as well go whole hog and fit an internal drive, which is more convenient (because it's contained inside the PC and accessed on the front of the PC) as well as being cheaper (because you don't have to pay extra money for the case that protects the drive). Nearly all PC CD-ROM drives have motorised trays, the only disadvantage of that being you can't get at a disc left in the machine while the PC is switched off.

Interface card

Not so much part of a specification as a necessity. You need an interface before you can connect up your CD-ROM drive. Briefly, there are three choices – a SCSI interface (only a viable option if you have one already or need one for something else apart from the CD-ROM drive), a 'proprietary' interface (designed specifically to connect one make of CD-ROM drive to a PC, which is not as good value) and a sound card (which can also act as a CD-ROM interface).

Sound card

The sound card fulfils three different functions. For starters, it can decode and play CD-DA (hi-fi CD quality) audio, and so sound cards almost always come with a software program that will enable your PC to play audio CDs. Secondly, it decodes and plays computer digital audio, which is slightly different from CD-DA. Thirdly, it also enables you to create your own digital sounds and music – sound cards often come with a microphone and sound sampling software. You'll also frequently get a pair of stereo headphones with a sound card.

TOP TIP

Modern sound cards use a 16-bit sound resolution, just like CD-DA, so are capable of creating CD-quality sounds. It is an advantage to buy a 16-bit card, rather than an older 8-bit sound card, and you should also look for a card that features stereo sound.

For the highest quality, look for a card that supports a sample rate of 44.1kHz, the same as CD-DA. Some cards can play back at this frequency but will only record (sample) sounds at half the rate, 22kHz, though that is still sufficient for most music sampling (and remember that the lower the sample rate, the less hard disk space a sampled sound will take up). An even lower rate of 11kHz is generally considered sufficient for sampled speech.

A sound card like this Gravis can also act as a CD-ROM drive interface. Sound card makers specify which models of CD-ROM drive their cards will support, and cards are often available in different versions that give different types of interfaces. Some even provide a SCSI interface.

Many sound cards also have highly advanced features for making your own music, because they effectively include a synthesiser on a chip which can generate its own sounds. Most use a Yamaha chip that's the equivalent of a cheap electronic keyboard, but more expensive models feature wave table sounds – digitised recordings of sounds from real instruments – and the quality is much better. But that really only becomes a factor if you're planning to play around with desktop music on your PC.

Many sound cards also feature a joystick interface, and some even come with a free joystick. Again for musicians, this joystick connector can sometimes also act as a MIDI interface (Musical Instrument Digital Interface), though normally you'll have to add an extra interface for controlling, or recording from, MIDI instruments.

TOP TIP

Finally, probably the most important thing to look for in a sound card is Sound Blaster compatibility.

The Sound Blaster, made by a firm called Creative Labs, was one of the very first PC sound cards and became a de facto standard for PC sounds. For that reason, most games and multimedia programs play their sounds expecting them to be interpreted by a Sound Blaster card. So in order to use these programs to the full, you need to have a sound card that is Sound Blaster compatible.

An added complication is that some sound cards are more Sound Blaster compatible than others, so even if you do get a card that says it's of the Sound Blaster standard, you might find that some software will not work with it. If you want to play safe, get a genuine Creative Labs Sound Blaster card.

Optional powered stereo speakers

If you have a good sound card, take full advantage of it with speakers. Get mains-powered speakers rather than battery-powered ones, and look for magnetic shielding which will mean you can put them next to the monitor without affecting the display.

Summary of minimum specification for PC CD-ROM

- **386SX minimum, but 486SX preferred**
- **4Mb RAM (preferably 8Mb)**
- **120Mb hard drive**
- **Microsoft-compatible mouse**
- **MS-DOS 6 and Windows 3**
- **256-colour SVGA monitor**
- **Window accelerated video card**
- **Sound Blaster-compatible sound card**
- **Double-speed CD-ROM drive**
- **Optional powered stereo speakers**

The MPC Level One standard

This is the older, outdated standard set by the MPC marketing Council, which was outdated and so had to be improved to MPC Level Two, overleaf.

- 386SX or higher processor
- 2Mb RAM
- 30Mb hard disk drive
- VGA or S-VGA display
- Two-button mouse
- 101-key keyboard
- CD-ROM drive with 150K/sec transfer rate (single speed) without consuming more than 40% of CPU time during the process; 1 second maximum average seek time; CD-DA output; Sub-channel Q support (for interleaved audio); MSCDEX 2.2 driver or equivalent.

The MPC Level Two standard

This is the new, updated Multimedia PC standard that in some respects sets unnecessary and over-ambitious specifications, but is a reliable guide to what to expect from a quality multimedia PC set-up.

- 25MHz 486SX
- 4Mb of RAM (8Mb recommended)
- 3.5-inch high-density (1.44Mb) floppy disk drive
- 160Mb hard drive
- VGA colour monitor with display resolution of 640 by 480 pixels with 65,536 colours (16-bit colour)
- 101-key IBM-style keyboard

- Two-button mouse
- Two serial ports, one for mouse and one free for comms
- Joystick port
- CD-ROM drive with 300K/sec transfer rate (double-speed); average seek time of 400 milliseconds (0.4 sec) or less; 10,000 hours MTBF (Mean Time Between Failure, or in other words, tested life expectancy); CD-ROM XA ready; multisession capable; subchannel Q support; CD-DA outputs (RCA audio outputs) and volume control on front panel.
- 16-bit sound card with microphone input; internal synthesiser capability (multi-voice, multi-timbral, eight channels comprising 6 simultaneous melody notes plus 2 percussion notes); internal mixing capabilities (for combining CD-DA and computer-generated audio and sending both to the speakers); MIDI I/O port for musical instruments.

Choosing and buying a new, complete multimedia PC

If you're starting from scratch, it's an awful lot easier to buy a complete, ready-to-go multimedia PC than it is to buy a base-specification model and upgrade it yourself. It's probably cheaper, it's certainly easier (because you don't have to do any fitting of hardware inside the PC case) and it means that if anything does stop working, you only have the one supplier to deal with.

One slightly frustrating aspect of looking through computer magazines for advice on buying a PC is that you seldom see specific advice that says "this is a good one, buy it." There's a good reason for that, though.

PCs are a combination of different parts – motherboard, case, hard drive and so on, and that's before you even consider the multimedia elements such as graphics card, sound card and CD-ROM drive – and PCs are very often put together not by a manufacturer, but by a supplier, who buys in all the components and builds them into a ready-to-buy PC. For this reason, exact specifications change rapidly.

As for where to buy, direct sellers (manufacturers who sell direct to the public rather than via a supplier) and mail order companies advertising in magazines are often able to offer the best prices.

If you are worried about buying something without actually seeing it first, remember that you have the right to return any goods bought by mail order. To take any risk out of the process, pay by credit card (which insures your purchase too) or look for a safeguard like the *PC Plus* magazine buyers' protection scheme, to take the worry out of the process.

PCs are now widely available in high street stores and a healthy degree of competition has built up between stores like Dixons, Comet, Currys and Tandy. Many department stores, such as John Lewis, now also have computer departments, though superstores like the PC World chain are usually able to offer wider choice and better prices.

Just as important as the initial price, though, are the warranty and the after-sales service. You would be well advised not to buy a computer from anywhere that you can't pop into or phone up for advice, hints and help when you need it, which makes friendly independent shops a good bet.

As for warranties, a 'back-to-base' arrangement means you have to send the machine back to its makers to be fixed, so if anything does go wrong, this can mean it's a long time before you get it back as well as proving costly in postage. A much better arrangement is an on-site repair warranty, which means an engineer will be sent to your house to fix or replace whatever's gone wrong. Extended guarantees can be rather expensive, so these are very much a personal decision, but some manufacturers offer a two-year on-site warranty with the initial purchase, and that's a pretty good deal.

Another option: the tower system

One last factor you might wish to consider when you're choosing a multimedia PC is the shape of the case. Normally PCs come in large boxes that take up a lot of desk space and really get in the way, and they also tend to have very loud cooling fans, the constant whine of which can get very annoying.

A good way of getting round both problems is to buy a PC in a tower configuration, which is effectively just a normal size and shape of PC, but turned on its side. Tower systems are designed to rest on the floor underneath the desk, with long cables for the keyboard, mouse and monitor, which are the only bits you then need on the disk.

As well as the PC being out of the way on the floor, the other advantage is that the noise of a loud fan tends to be a good deal less intrusive when it's at ankle level and not amplified by the resonant surface of a desk.

PCs in a tower system configuration are often available as an option at no extra cost.

Multimedia upgrade kits for the PC

An upgrade kit contains the two basic elements needed to turn a normal PC into a CD-ROM powered multimedia machine – a sound card (acting as CD-ROM interface) and the CD-ROM drive itself – as well as a few extras, such as powered stereo speakers, joystick,

Here's a multimedia upgrade kit ready to go into the PC's box. Note the sound card, CD-ROM drive, instructions manual and bundled software.

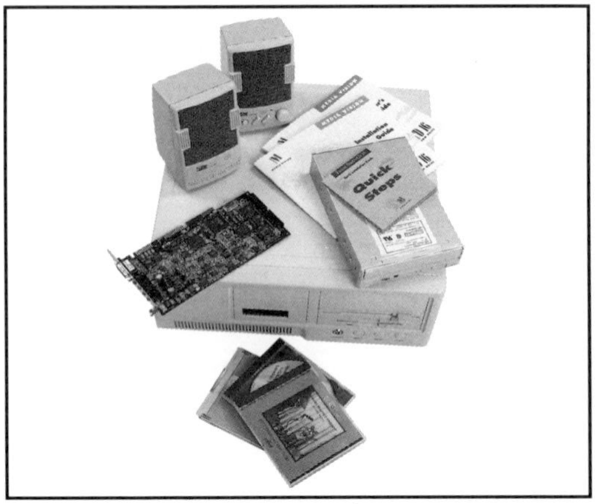

microphone and headphones, and also very often a range of CD-ROM software titles.

If you've got a decent PC already, you may not even need this much. If you had a good gamesplaying PC set-up, for instance, such as a 486SX with 4Mb of RAM, 160Mb hard drive, Super VGA card and Sound Blaster Pro card, all you would need to buy in addition would be a Mitsumi or Panasonic CD-ROM drive, both of which can connect up to the sound card, and you can have a CD-ROM system for only an extra £150 or so.

On the other hand, you might need a lot more than the upgrade kit can offer. If you have a 386SX with 2Mb of RAM, a small hard drive and only VGA graphics capability, you will have to spend a lot of money improving that lot before you even start to add the multimedia upgrade kit, so it might be worth considering starting again with a new machine.

However, there are many cases in which the upgrade kit will suit perfectly. The advantage of buying all the pieces in an all-in-one pack like this is that you generally pay about the same as you would for a separate CD-ROM drive and sound card, and you end up with all the other bits effectively for free.

The most valuable part of the deal is likely to be the CD-ROM software, which will very often include expensive items like encyclopedias. So it can actually be wise to shop around with the bundled software as the main factor that influences your decision.

Chapter 6
Getting started with CD-ROM

- Installing a drive and driver software
- Tips for using your CD-ROM drive
- Installing CD-ROM software
- Solving memory problems
- Tidying up hard drives

Introduction

Well, we're getting pretty warm. If you've looked carefully through the preceding few chapters you should know all about how CD-ROM drives work and what type to buy, and you should also have decided on a Mac or PC CD-ROM set-up that will suit you. The last remaining piece in the puzzle is to fit and run your CD-ROM drive.

So to kick off this chapter, that's exactly what we'll do. Installing a Mac CD-ROM drive is usually just a matter of plugging it in, but the PC drive will generally be an internally fitted unit that requires you to take off the lid of your PC and play around inside. We'll show you how.

We'll also be looking at the software that you will need to install onto your hard drive to make the CD-ROM drive work, and looking at the solutions to a few common problems that you might have when you're just starting out with a CD-ROM drive.

Fitting a Mac CD-ROM drive

As we've already said, the most common form of Mac CD-ROM drive is an external drive like the AppleCD 300, so actually plugging in and setting up is simplicity itself. Provided you don't have any other SCSI devices attached, all you have to do is the following.

WARNING

1. Shut down your Mac and switch everything off. You should never plug in or unplug anything while the Mac is switched on.

2. Connect the cable to the SCSI input connector on the back of the CD-ROM drive. The end of the cable that goes in the drive is the one with the larger plug on it (the plug has a row of large gold-coloured 'teeth' inside it). Note that the plug is longer along the top, so you can't fit it upside down, and push it home gently, keeping it

level and square to the drive. Then secure it in place by pressing in the wire clips on either side of the socket so that they click into place. Generally, you'll connect the cable to the lower one of the two sockets on the back of the CD-ROM drive.

3. If there is not one already in place, you will need to attach a SCSI terminator (a kind of blanking plug) to the other, top SCSI socket on the CD-ROM drive.

4. Connect the other end of the cable to the SCSI port on the back of the Apple Macintosh (the connector is identified by a diamond-shaped symbol, but the SCSI cable plug won't go into any of the others, so you can't get it wrong anyway). Again, note that the plug is longer along the top, so you can't fit it upside down, and push it home gently, keeping it level and square to the Mac. Then secure it in place by screwing in the two retaining screws.

5. Plug the 'kettle'-style power lead into a wall socket and into the back of the CD-ROM drive, then switch on the CD drive using the power switch at the back. Now power the Mac up, and install the software provided on the Install floppy disk that comes with the CD-ROM drive.

WARNING

Remember – you should always switch on all peripherals, including CD-ROM drive, monitor and printer, before you switch on the Mac. And conversely, always shut down the Mac (which parks the drive heads in the hard disk drive, making your data safer) and switch it off before you switch off all the other peripherals.

If you're fitting a CD-ROM drive to a Mac yourself, it will most likely be an external drive like this one, which basically only needs to be plugged in.

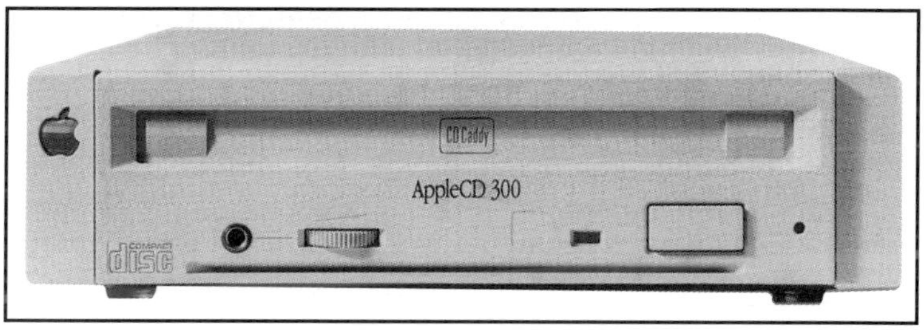

If you already have other SCSI devices operating...

If you have other SCSI devices already in operation, you will need to remove the terminator from the last one and fit the CD-ROM drive on the end of the chain, attaching the SCSI terminator to it.

You may have to alter the SCSI device number, if it clashes with one of the SCSI peripherals you already have attached. Each SCSI device in the chain must be identified by a different number between 1 and 6, so that the Mac does not mix them up.

You can change the SCSI number of any peripheral by finding the small counter on the back of the device, which will have a small button above and below it. Pushing the button above the counter will increase the SCSI ID number, while pushing the button below will decrease it.

You may need to use a SCSI mounting program like *SCSI Probe* to tell your Macintosh the new ID numbers of the various SCSI devices in your chain.

Installing a PC CD-ROM drive

Generally, an add-on CD-ROM drive for the PC will be fitted inside the computer's case. Playing around inside your PC is really not as difficult or as daunting as it might first appear, provided you use a little common sense, patience and care, and you follow the rules.

PCs are designed with big boxes and extra slots that can accommodate extra cards, so you are expected to take the lid off and fit something during the lifetime of your PC, and therefore it's not too complicated.

Check before you buy

Before you actually buy an upgrade kit, it's a good idea to check a couple of simple things.

TOP TIP

Even if your PC seems to have a spare 5.25-inch drive bay to fit the drive into, take the cover off and check that the bay is not already filled up: some models of PC put the hard disk drive in this space. If that's the case, you'll need to buy an external CD-ROM drive instead.

Check to make sure that your PC has a spare 8-bit or 16-bit slot, as appropriate, to fit your sound card into. If you are planning to use a separate CD-ROM drive interface card as a controller instead of using the sound card, then you will need two slots, one for each.

Some budget PCs use a cheap power supply that is barely adequate, so check that the power rating of the power supply will cope when you add on the needs of a CD-ROM drive.

And some sound cards rely on hardware 'jumper' links to set the IRQ (Interrupt Request) numbers which identify the devices attached to the PC, including the sound card and CD-ROM drive. Check your handbook to see if this must be done before you put the PC's case back together.

Extra preparation

There's a couple of other things you might like to have to hand before you start work.

TOP TIP

If the PC is going to be moved around a lot, it's a good idea to fix all the connectors in place with silicon rubber compound after you've fitted the CD-ROM drive and checked that everything works – so buy a tube of the appropriate compound.

The surest way to guard against static electricity sparking from your body and harming chips inside the PC is to wear electrician's anti-static wristbands, which are available quite cheaply from good electronics shops.

Finally, the only other pieces of equipment you'll need are a couple of screwdrivers and your bare hands.

Fitting the CD-ROM drive

Here's a simple, illustrated, step-by-step guide to the process of fitting the CD-ROM drive inside your PC.

1. Some PC components are sensitive to static shock, so your first move should always be to earth yourself by touching some substantial metal object. The PC must be plugged in, but must be switched off. Once you've earthed yourself you must unplug the computer from the mains to avoid getting electrocuted. Now remove the screws that hold the cover on, slide the cover off, and put it somewhere out of the way.

2. Choose an empty 5.25-inch drive bay where the CD-ROM drive is going to sit, and prise off the dummy cover plate. The easiest way to do this is generally to use a screwdriver to bend back the clips that hold the blanking plate in place, while gently easing off the plate.

3. With some PC designs, the cage for the hard and floppy disk drives will obscure the screw holes that you need for the screws that hold the CD-ROM drive in place. If this is the case, then unscrew and remove the cage – hard disk drives are fragile, so move it gently – and carefully rest the cage on another part of the PC's case, to hold it out of the way while you gain access to the screw holes.

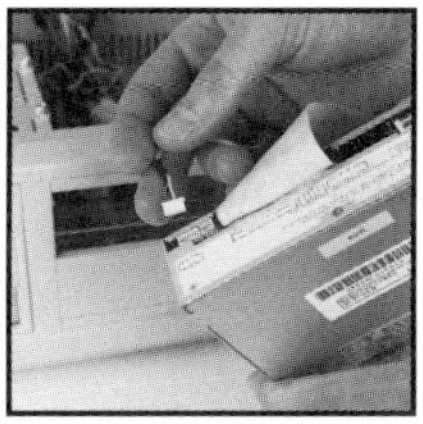

4. Connect the ribbon cable that comes from the sound card or interface card and controls the CD-ROM drive to the back of the drive unit. Some will also have a cable for playing normal audio CDs through the sound card. The connectors are usually designed so you can't fit them the wrong way round, so don't try to force them into place.

5. Slide the CD-ROM drive into place in the drive bay, then find a spare 4-way connector from the power supply and connect it to the CD-ROM drive. Now line up the CD-ROM drive so it is flush with the front of the PC case, and screw it in to the drive bay. Check that none of the connectors are squeezed, pinched or bent awkwardly.

6. Connect the other end of the controlling ribbon cable to the sound card or the interface card that you are using to control the CD-ROM drive. If you are using a sound card, don't forget to plug in the audio cable as well, for playing audio CDs.

7. Pick out a spare slot and slot in the sound card or interface card. Most modern sound cards are 16-bit, so you'll need one of the 16-bit slots. You can identify them easily, because the 8-bit slots are only half the length. Replace the PC case cover, reconnect all the leads (power, monitor etc) and refer to your instruction manual for how to go about installing the driver software to make your CD-ROM drive work.

Installing the driver software on your Mac

Fortunately this is usually extremely simple, because all you need to do is stick the Install disk in the floppy disk drive and double-click the Install program to run it – it does the rest automatically.

However, to understand what's going on better, and just in case you need to poke around your System folder and locate all the necessary bits of software, here's a run-down of what goes where and does what.

Incidentally, if you make a back-up of these files on a floppy disk and need to re-install them, all you have to do is select all the files drag them over your closed System folder. The System 7 Finder will sort out which are Extensions, Control Panels or Apple Menu Items, and put them all in the appropriate folder inside the System folder.

Just to give you an idea of a typical case, here's a quick run-through of the files related to CD-ROMs that I've found installed in my system folder, and what they do.

Apple menu items

CD Remote – this is the standard Apple software for playing CD-ROM discs, which is pretty basic and functional and will run in the background, playing an audio CD for you to listen to while you work using hard disk-based software.

Control panels

AppleCD Speed Switch – an AppleCD 300 program used for switching from double-speed to single-speed, so as to play audio CDs etc.

Extensions

- Apple CD-ROM – CD-ROM driver for this particular model.
- CD Remote init – driver for audio CD playing.

The drivers for your CD-ROM drive belong in the System Extensions folder, but you will also install programs to control your CD-ROM drive in the Apple Menu Items and Control Panels folders of your Macintosh.

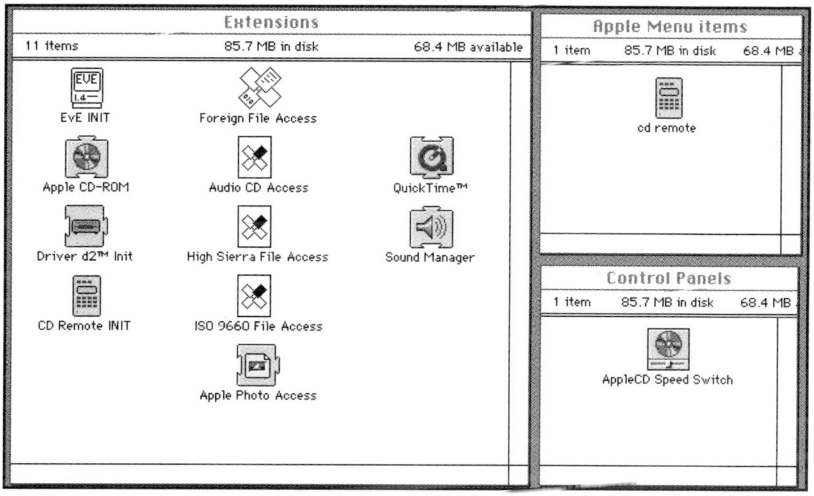

- Foreign File Access – general interpreter for reading other CD-ROM file formats besides Apple HFS.

- High Sierra File Access – specific interpreter for accessing High Sierra format (CD-ROM XA).

- ISO 9660 File Access – specific interpreter for accessing ISO9660 discs (PC CD-ROMs).

- Audio CD Access – specific interpreter for accessing audio CDs (CD-DA).

- Apple Photo Access – interpreter that enables the Mac to read Kodak Photo CD discs.

Sound Manager – alternative handler for Mac 'beep' sounds which is used by a lot of CD-ROM software. If you need it to run a CD-ROM disc, a copy of the program will be included on the disc and you can install it by dragging it on to the closed System folder.

QuickTime – the run-time version of the software that enables the Mac to play data-compressed video clips. Again, if you need

QuickTime to run the videos on a CD-ROM disc, a copy of the program will be included on the disc and you can install it by dragging it on to the closed System folder.

Installing the driver software on a PC

Generally, you will only need to run an install program program from floppy disk which will install all the necessary drivers for you – so it's just a question of navigating your way to the right path and typing the right command in DOS, or using the Windows menu to Browse, find and Run the right executable. Falling off a log stuff.

What the install program will do is copy the CD-ROM drivers to your hard disk drive and put them in the start-up area of the hard drive, usually the DOS folder. It will also install the MS-DOS CD-ROM file-handling extension MSCDEX.EXE. And it will usually also modify the files that the PC reads to set up its operations when it starts up, the autoexec.bat and config.sys files.

In most circumstances, all the operations should be carried out for you automatically, so that you don't need to get your hands dirty doing it manually, but it is useful to know what goes on and how to do it yourself, if only so that you understand your multimedia PC better – so here's how it all works.

MSCDEX.EXE and your proprietary CD-ROM driver

Previously, MS-DOS could only handle files of a maximum size of 32Mb, but for the purposes of CD-ROM this is not good enough. For that reason, Microsoft created an extension program that modifies MS-DOS's file handling when you use a CD-ROM, and this program is called Microsoft CD Extension, shortened for DOS filename purposes to MSCDEX.EXE (the .EXE on the end of the name showing that it is an executable file – a program).

Both this and the specific device driver for your make and model of CD-ROM drive (which is also an executable file) must be copied to your hard disk drive – usually C: – and installed in the DOS folder (C:\DOS) where they are readily available for access.

Modifying config.sys and autoexec.bat

These start-up files are very important, and before you modify them you should always make a back-up copy (and preferably also a copy on a self-booting floppy disk) so that if anything goes wrong with your modifications you can boot up your PC and repair the damage.

Having said that, so long as you type carefully you shouldn't be able to mess things up. To modify either of the files, you need to use the Editor program which is built in to MS-DOS, which you can load simply by typing EDIT at the DOS prompt.

First, you'll need to load and change the config.sys file, which is located in the root directory of your start-up hard disk drive. You'll now need to refer to the picture here of a typical config.sys file for the rest of this to make sense.

The first line you'll need to change is the LASTDRIVE command, which is about six lines down. This command is used to tell MS-DOS how many of the 26 letters of the alphabet you want to use to describe devices. Normally a PC will have floppy disk drives A: and B: as well as a hard drive with the device name C: so the command will probably read LASTDRIVE=C. Normally your CD-ROM drive will be called D: and you won't have any further devices after that, so you can modify the command to read LASTDRIVE=D. Our example system has a second hard disk drive, and so the CD-ROM drive is set up as E:.

The other line you need to notice is the device specification line for the CD-ROM drive, which in our example is the second (the middle

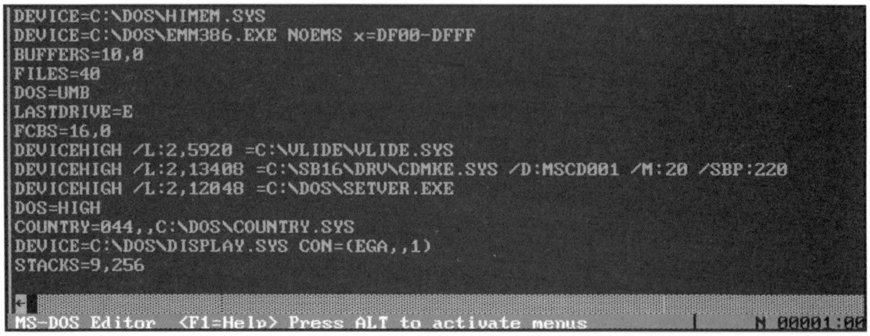

```
DEVICE=C:\DOS\HIMEM.SYS
DEVICE=C:\DOS\EMM386.EXE NOEMS x=DF00-DFFF
BUFFERS=10,0
FILES=40
DOS=UMB
LASTDRIVE=E
FCBS=16,0
DEVICEHIGH /L:2,5920 =C:\VLIDE\VLIDE.SYS
DEVICEHIGH /L:2,13408 =C:\SB16\DRV\CDMKE.SYS /D:MSCD001 /M:20 /SBP:220
DEVICEHIGH /L:2,12048 =C:\DOS\SETVER.EXE
DOS=HIGH
COUNTRY=044,,C:\DOS\COUNTRY.SYS
DEVICE=C:\DOS\DISPLAY.SYS CON=(EGA,,1)
STACKS=9,256

MS-DOS Editor  <F1=Help> Press ALT to activate menus        N 00001:00
```

Here's an example CONFIG.SYS file, loaded into the Editor program. Refer to this screenshot while reading the text.

one) of the three lines near the bottom that start with the DEVICEHIGH command.

These lines are all telling the system to run different device drivers, which is what the DEVICEHIGH bit means. The /L modifier which comes first after the DEVICEHIGH command normally specifies the device letter, but ours is set up a slightly different way – don't worry about that.

The most important bit comes next in the line, with =C:\SB16\DRV\CDMKE.SYS. This is the path and name of our CD-ROM driver: the driver is actually called CDMKE.SYS and because we're using a Sound Blaster 16 sound card as an interface, the driver is located in a driver folder (DRV) in the Sound Blaster software folder (SB16) on the hard disk drive C:.

The other modifiers specify other details of the way the driver is run. The /D modifier tells the system to set up a file called MSCD001 which will contain information about the CD-ROM drive, and this file is also referred to in the autoexec.bat file. The /M modifier tells the system to allocate 20 buffers of memory to the drive, which means 40K will be used as a buffer. The /SBP modifier is specific to the sound Blaster driver, so don't worry about that one.

The instruction manual for your CD-ROM drive will help you to type in the right instructions in the DEVICE command line. You

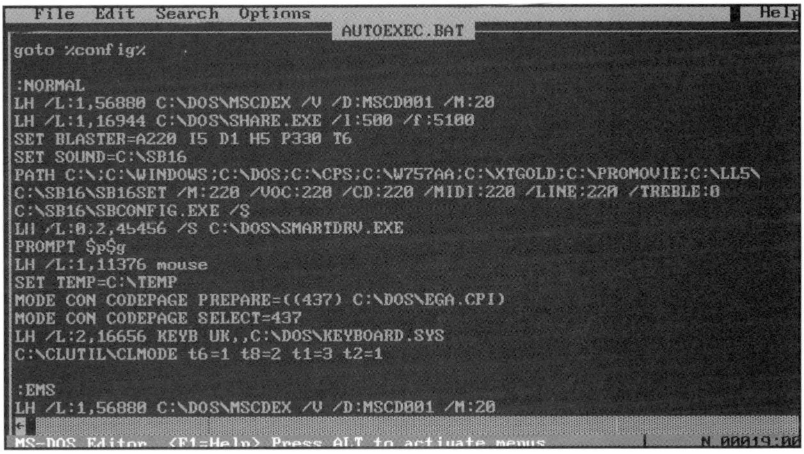

Here's our autoexec.bat file, loaded into the Editor program. Again, you need to refer to this picture when reading the text.

must now save the config.sys file before you open the autoexec.bat file.

Again, we've included a screen grab of a sample autoexec.bat file here for you to refer to. The important line here is the third one down, the one that comes after the line which just says NORMAL on it.

The first part of the line (LH /L:1,56880) is specific to the way we're handling the memory on our example PC, so don't worry about that bit. The important part is rest of the line, which will look pretty much the same as this in all PC autoexec.bat files.

The first part – C:\DOS\MSCDEX – tells the system where to find MSCDEX.EXE, and also tells the system to run it. The /D:MSCD001 modifier tells MSCDEX.EXE what the name of the file created by your CD-ROM driver is, so that the two programs can co-operate in using this file. The /M:20 modifier tells MSCDEX.EXE to use 40K of RAM as a buffer for the drive. Finally, we also slipped in a /V modifier which tells MSCDEX.EXE to send information about memory use to the screen display, so we can see what it's doing.

With this line in place, your autoexec.bat file is all ready to use, so save it and exit the Editor program.

The changes you have made to the two start-up files will not take effect until you restart the PC, so to use your newly configured CD-ROM drive you must now switch the PC off for a few seconds and then restart.

Other software

As well as the bare necessities of the drivers, you will usually get quite a lot of other software with the CD-ROM drive, especially if you're using a sound card as your CD-ROM interface, in which case you'll probably have all sorts of interesting sound sampling software. The thing that might interest you most at first, however, might be the audio CD player program that you will almost certainly now find installed in a Windows directory, waiting for you to try it out!

Tips for using your CD-ROM drive

CD-ROM drives are pretty simple things, and so you shouldn't have any problem at all using yours: but here are some points to bear in mind.

- **Mac CD-ROM discs are handled by the Finder in just the same way as floppy disks are, which means that the Eject is handled by software rather than being a physical operation. Drag the CD-ROM disc's icon to the Wastebasket and the disc, in its caddy, will be ejected. The Mac will also eject the disc when you shut down or switch off your Mac.**

- **You may notice that the Mac often takes a while to check the CD-ROM disc and display an icon on the screen after you've put the caddy in the CD-ROM drive. This is perfectly normal.**

- Most PC CD-ROM drives use tray-loading systems that require power, so you won't be able to eject a disc you've left in the drive without switching the PC on.

- A PC CD-ROM drive will need to be given a few seconds to look at the disc and recognise it before it will do anything with the disc. Watch for the drive light to go out before you expect File Manager or an application to be able to read from a disc.

- Some PC applications will crash if you take out a disc while the application is running. To be on the safe side, quit the application before removing the disc.

- The most common reason for a CD not working is that you've done something really dumb like put a Mac disc in a PC, or put the disc in the drive with the data side up and the label side down. Don't worry, we all do it – but learn the lesson that if something goes wrong, you should always check the simplest things first.

WARNING

Never run an external CD-ROM drive standing on its side or upside-down – always keep it the right way up.

- CD-ROM drives, like CD players, are simple devices and don't require any maintenance. But do keep the disc tray (platen) or caddy clean and free of dust, and keep it closed when not in use.

Installing CD-ROM software

Some CD-ROM software will run purely from the disc, but most of it requires you to install a controller program and often some data files, too, onto the hard disk drive of your PC or Mac. These files vary in size, and can be anything from a few hundred K to 10Mb or more.

The reason why these files need to be on the hard drive is pretty simple. Take an obvious example like an encyclopedia.

The encyclopedia disc will contain thousands of entries and millions of words, but you need to be able to search through them as quickly as possible to find what you want. Because the hard drive can access data so much faster than the CD-ROM drive, the encyclopedia application installed on the hard drive will include an index of all the topics, so it can quickly pick out any entries you have asked it to search for.

You can then browse through the entries the search has picked out at your leisure, and the load time from CD-ROM that is needed to display each individual article is a lot less noticeable and intrusive.

Nearly all CD-ROM applications have data files that the program needs to use all the time, and of course the control programs for the disc run more quickly from a hard drive too, so nearly all CD-ROM discs require you to install a few files onto your hard drive.

Windows programs, of course, need to create an icon on your desktop to run the program from and so absolutely all Windows CD-ROM discs will require you to run an install procedure, even if it only creates a workgroup and an icon so that you can run the software.

Installing Mac CD-ROM software

With all Mac discs, you start off the same way. Put the disc in the caddy and put it in the drive, and an icon will appear on the desktop. Sometimes you will have to double-click the icon to open a disc window, and sometimes the disc window will pop up automatically for you.

Usually you will now see a collection of icons in the disc window, including the main application as well as data file and folders, and very often a 'Read Me' file. Double-click on the Read Me file and you may get instructions on what to do next.

In some cases no install procedure is necessary, and all you have to do now is double-click on the application icon to run the program.

In other cases you will only have to install the main application, which you do simply by dragging its icon from the disc window onto the icon for your hard drive. This will put the application in the top directory of your hard drive, but there's nothing to stop you from putting the application in any folder, anywhere you want, on your hard drive – it will still work.

Sometimes you can also speed up the operation of the application by putting some data files onto the hard drive, too. Again, all you need to do is drag them across and put them where you want.

Occasionally you will also have to install some extra software on your Mac before an application can operate. Normally this will either be a System Extension, such as QuickTime or Sound Manager, or a specific font used by text in the screens of the program. In these cases, simply drag the icons on top of your closed System folder, and the Mac will automatically put them in the right places in the System.

If you already have them then you don't need to do this, but you can check to see if the ones on the disc are newer versions. Do this by selecting the icon and pressing Command-I for information, and comparing the version numbers.

Less commonly, you may have to copy an application program such as HyperCard onto your Mac hard drive before a CD-ROM application will work, but again all you need to do is drag it to anywhere on your hard drive that you want.

Finally, a rare few Mac CD-ROM applications have an Install procedure which you run by double-clicking an icon, and very

Installing a typical CD-ROM application on the Mac. A control program file and a folder of data files need to be copied onto the hard disk. Usually you have to drag them over the hard disk manually, but some programs, like the one shown here, will install all necessary items for you.

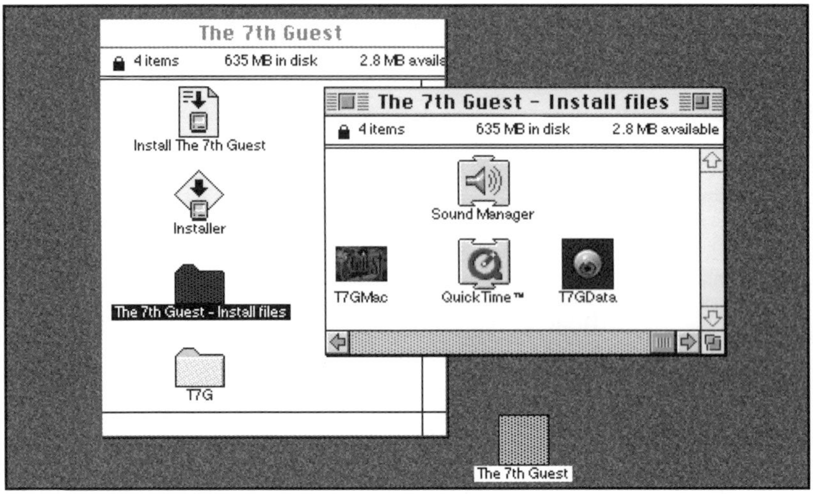

occasionally this Install program will be contained on a separate floppy disk. Installers are simplicity itself: they may prompt you to make certain choices, but the Install routine will copy everything you need onto your hard drive, and put it all in the right places.

Installing DOS CD-ROM software on a PC

DOS software installation tends to be a little more intimidating, because it requires you to type a few commands. However, almost all DOS install procedures only get you to run an install routine, which will then do the rest of the work for you.

The instructions are usually printed clearly both in the manual and on the card that slips into the CD jewel case. You'll generally only have to change to the CD-ROM drive (by typing CD D:) and then type INSTALL or SETUP or similar command to run the install routine.

This will then normally create a directory on your hard disk drive and copy all the files it needs into this directory. To run the program, you will then have to change to this new directory (though the install routine often does this for you as well) and type the name of the program.

One warning: some DOS install routines will want to change your start-up configurations (config.sys or autoexec.bat), generally because the program doesn't agree with your sound card set-up. Usually the install program will ask if this is OK – think twice about saying yes. It's better to have the application running without sound than it is to have your set-up messed around with, especially if you don't know how to put it straight again.

Installing Windows CD-ROM software on a PC

I have yet to come across a Windows disc that works in any way but one, and that's by running an install routine called SETUP, or something similar.

All you have to do is select the Run option from the file menu and either just type D:SETUP or use the Browse option to pick out the CD-ROM drive and select the file called SETUP.EXE from the list. Then click on OK, and the install routine will run.

Usually all the install routine will need you to do along the way is confirm its choice of name and location for a new directory on the hard drive for it to store its data in. Some install procedures also go into other, important directories on your hard disk drive in order to add other Windows extensions, such as the run-time version of Video for Windows or the PC version of QuickTime.

Very often the install routine will want to restart Windows in order for changes it has made to take effect. That's fine, so long as you don't have any other Windows programs running with unsaved data in, in which case say no, sort out your other applications, then close and restart Windows yourself.

Macintosh memory tips

Mac CD-ROM applications tend to want an awful lot of RAM, but System 7 uses a lot itself, so if you're running demanding CD-ROM titles on a 4Mb machine you might find that some will refuse to run. Here's a few tips on how to squeeze the most out of 4Mb.

- **Switch the Mac off and leave it off for about a minute to clear the RAM out thoroughly.**
- **Use the About This Macintosh option from the Apple menu to keep a check on how much memory is being used.**
- **Pare your system down to a minimum by getting rid of all unnecessary System Extensions and inits. You should be able to run a System as little as 1400K.**
- **Check that only Finder and your CD-ROM application are running.**
- **If the CD-ROM control program is copied to your hard drive, select its icon and use the Command-I key combination to Get Information. In the window that opens, you can now adjust the program's memory usage right down to the specified minimum.**
- **Check that your clipboard doesn't contain any large items (the clipboard is held in RAM). Clear it by copying a single letter from a file name.**
- **Use the Memory Control Panel to set the hard disk cache as small as possible.**
- **If all else fails, use the Memory Control Panel to set up a massive chunk of virtual memory (hard disk space that is used as a temporary storage area, pretending it is RAM). Your CD-ROM application will run incredibly, painfully slowly, but at least it will run!**

(This will only work on a Mac equipped with a 68030 CPU or above, and only if you're using System 7.)

PC memory tips

The Windows PC is much more economical with memory than a Mac and better at using it so you shouldn't generally run out of RAM altogether. However, there are two things to note.

MAKE A NOTE!

Both Windows 3.0 and 3.1 have a bug which means that Windows will sometimes say it has run out of memory even when it has stacks left to play with. The only thing you can do is quit all applications that you're not using and if that doesn't work quit out of Windows and restart.

Because of the way the PC has developed over the years, it retains a peculiar way of organising its memory that separates off the first 640K as 'conventional memory', and organises the rest as either 'expanded memory' or 'extended memory'. Certain CD-ROM applications, especially games, insist on using one of these two types and not the other, which can make life difficult. The solution is just as complicated as the problem. To explain it in full, we've included a separate section on how it works – and it's coming up next!

Dealing with different types of PC memory

First, the background. In the early days of the PC, more than ten years ago, when computers were a lot more primitive, 256K of RAM was an incredibly vast amount of memory. Times changed, PCs got more powerful, but after a while poor old DOS, the PC's basic operating system, got stuck in a timewarp. It managed to get as far as using 640K of memory, but couldn't get any further.

When 286 PCs came along and wanted to use 2Mb or more of RAM, a half-baked solution was cooked up. The original 640K was set aside and called 'conventional memory', and modifications were made that allowed programs to access, indirectly, all the extra RAM. All the memory between 640K and 1Mb was labelled 'high memory', and anything above that was defined as 'expanded memory' and accessed by a system called EMS.

When 386 and 486 PCs came along, they did things differently. They used a new system which referred to all memory above 1Mb as extended memory, and this was accessed using a system called XMS. And so the scene was set for the memory complications of today.

Running out of conventional memory

By far the commonest problem with running out of RAM is not having enough conventional memory, because of the 640K limit. Not only must DOS occupy this part of the RAM, but also device drivers for mouse, hard drives and CD-ROM drives need to use it as well, which leaves little room for programs to run in.

MS-DOS 5 brought a solution, with the ability to load both DOS and the device drivers into high memory. All you have to do is specify in the config.sys and autoexec.bat start-up files where you want everything to go.

It still didn't work perfectly, though, because some devices would try to use the same bits of RAM at the same time. MS-DOS 6 features a utility called MEMMAKER which is much better at organising memory properly, but you can also buy an extra application to do that organising job, such as Quarterdeck's QEMM, which gives excellent results.

EMS not XMS

The other major problem with PC memory-handling is that some CD-ROM applications which run from DOS, including not just a few but the vast majority of games, want to use expanded memory (EMS) rather than extended memory (XMS).

Fortunately, MS-DOS also now has the ability to set up the XMS of a modern PC so that it behaves like EMS, which you again specify in the config.sys and autoexec.bat start-up files, and that does solve the problem. The only trouble is that if you set up large quantities of your memory to behave as EMS, so satisfying the requirements of the games, you then run out of XMS for the other applications to use. Oh dear.

The only way round the problem is very simple but a bit of a pain, and that's to have two alternative sets of start up files: one which sets up lots of EMS especially for games software to use, and one which leaves all the RAM as XMS for the other programs to run in. You can then choose which one to use when you start your PC up, though it does mean you have to restart your PC every time you want to use a different kind of application.

The one thing that at least makes it slightly less of a pain is that MS-DOS 6 enables you to have alternative start-up files, and you can even write your start-up so that you get a menu on the screen when you first switch on your PC, and you can choose which of the two types of start-up you want to run.

We won't explain how to do this here, because this is neither the time nor the place for a detailed DOS tutorial: but we have included pictures showing listings for both config.sys and autoexec.bat files which we have set up on one of our PCs to work in this way, and examining these should show you how it's done.

With MS-DOS 6 you can easily set up a menu that appears when your PC starts up, from which you can choose to run either with a lot of EMS memory, which is needed by games software, or with a lot of XMS memory which is more normal.

```
 File  Edit  Search  Options                                        Help
                              CONFIG.SYS
[menu]
menuitem=NORMAL, Normal
menuitem=EMS, Use EMS
menucolor=15,1

[NORMAL]
DEVICE=C:\DOS\HIMEM.SYS
DEVICE=C:\DOS\EMM386.EXE NOEMS x=DF00-DFFF
BUFFERS=10,0
FILES=40
DOS=UMB
LASTDRIVE=E
FCBS=16,0
DEVICEHIGH /L:2,5920 =C:\VLIDE\VLIDE.SYS
DEVICEHIGH /L:2,13408 =C:\SB16\DRV\CDMKE.SYS /D:MSCD001 /M:20 /SBP:220
DEVICEHIGH /L:2,12048 =C:\DOS\SETVER.EXE
DOS=HIGH
COUNTRY=044,,C:\DOS\COUNTRY.SYS
DEVICE=C:\DOS\DISPLAY.SYS CON=(EGA,,1)
STACKS=9,256
[EMS]
DEVICE=C:\DOS\HIMEM.SYS
DEVICE=C:\DOS\EMM386.EXE RAM x=DF00-DFFF
BUFFERS=10,0
FILES=40
DOS=UMB
LASTDRIVE=E
FCBS=16,0
DEVICEHIGH /L:1,5920 =C:\VLIDE\VLIDE.SYS
DEVICEHIGH /L:1,13408 =C:\SB16\DRV\CDMKE.SYS /D:MSCD001 /M:20 /SBP:220
DEVICEHIGH /L:1,12048 =C:\DOS\SETVER.EXE
DOS=HIGH
COUNTRY=044,,C:\DOS\COUNTRY.SYS
rem DEVICE=C:\DOS\DISPLAY.SYS CON=(EGA,,1)
STACKS=9,256
```

Keeping your hard drive tidy

If you use a lot of different CD-ROM discs, and also if you try out a lot of the demos from discs that you've acquired from the covers of magazines, you may well find your hard disk filling up with all sorts of unwanted files.

Obviously it's a good idea to get rid of the ones that you're never going to use again, so make it a regular habit to have a clean-out and delete stuff you don't need. Some discs you will use frequently, so you'll want to leave the Windows group or the Mac control program on your hard drive for easy access. Other discs, though, you might only use once in a blue moon, so it's better to spend a couple of minutes installing it when you want to use it than it is to have lots of unused files clogging up your hard drive all the time.

On the PC, you'll find that software is pretty well behaved and won't leave lots of messy preferences files all over the place. Use File Manager to delete the directories created by both DOS and Windows applications, along with the data, program and preference files that the directories contain. On the Windows desktop, select and delete unwanted program and workgroup icons.

On the Mac, you will find it easy to get rid of program and data files, but you'll also discover lots of other stuff has been left lying around too. Look in the System folder itself and in the Preferences folder inside the System folder, and you'll find lots of preferences files set up by CD-ROM applications that you don't even remember using. Trash them. Look in the Fonts folder, and you'll discover all sorts of

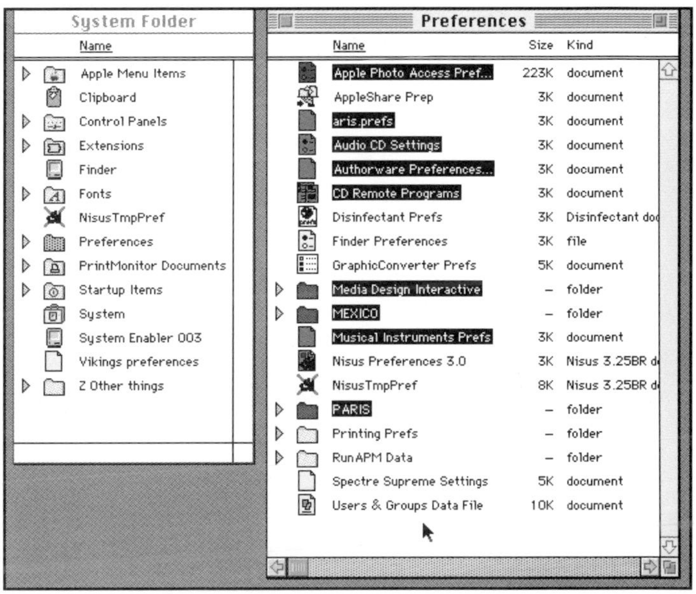

Keeping your Mac hard disk tidy: all the files highlighted here are preferences which have been created by Cd-ROM applications. If you are using a CD-ROM disc frequently then of course you'll want to leave its preferences file intact, but you may well find the Preferences folder full of files created by programs you'll never use again. You'll also very likely find lots of fonts on your Mac which have been put there by CD-ROM applications, and you'll probably want to get rid of most of those too.

extraneous typefaces littering the place which have been installed by CD-ROM applications – get rid of those as well.

On both the PC and Mac, when you've finished tidying up your hard drive you may find it's a good idea to run a defragmentation utility. This will close up all the small gaps left by small files that you've deleted and put back into one whole piece files that have previously been split and spread around the disc. Defragging will not only reduce the amount of hard disk space your data takes up by as much as a third, it will also considerably speed up your disk access times.

Chapter 7
Introducing multimedia

- What is multimedia?
- Important conventions of multimedia
- Typical multimedia applications
- Video standards

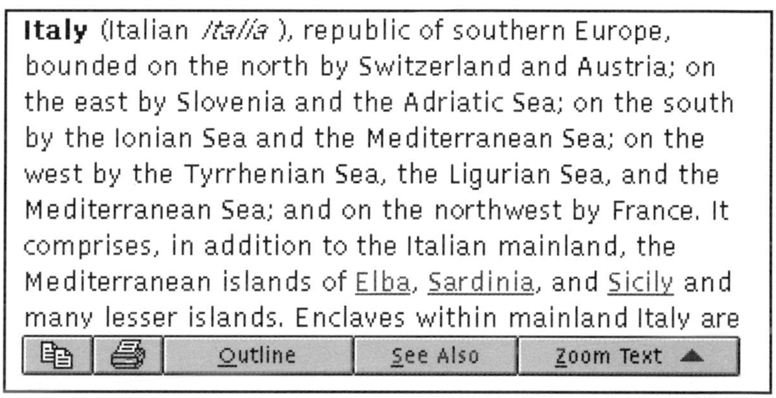

One of the conventions of interactive multimedia is hypertext. When you click on the red words in Encarta, for instance, you're taken down a new path to further information.

Introduction

The word 'multimedia' seems to be everywhere nowadays. You can buy a multimedia PC, use it to play a multimedia encyclopedia and then, when you want to take a break from your computer, pop down to your local art gallery to see a multimedia installation. It all gets rather confusing. In each of these contexts, the word has a slightly different meaning.

A historical definition of multimedia

The word 'multimedia' is a compound of the Latin prefix 'multi', meaning 'many', and the Latin-derived word 'media', which is the plural of the word medium. So multimedia simply means 'using more than one kind of medium'.

A medium, in this context, is any method used to deliver information. For an artist, watercolour is a medium, as are oil paint and gouache. In everyday usage, 'the media' are newspapers, magazines, television and radio.

By extension, the word medium is also used to mean any physical means that is used to store or distribute information. We all have a wide range of different media available to us in the home – ink on paper, audio tape, audio CDs, videotape and so on.

When the word multimedia first started being used in computing, it generally meant combining a computer with these older media: so a computer might be used to display text and pictures and also to control a videotape recorder, laserdisc player, or audio tape. But with the arrival of CD-ROM, the computer can now do it all...

CD-ROM multimedia

CD-ROM can be used to present information in all sorts of different ways, some of which – video and hi-fi quality music, for example – could not previously have been offered by a computer. A multimedia CD-ROM, therefore, is one that uses some or all of these different ways of presenting information:

- **Text**
- **Photographs**
- **Diagrams and illustrations**
- **Animation**
- **Video**
- **Narration**
- **Sound recordings**
- **Music**

Over the last few years, the people who create and publish multimedia CD-ROMs have been experimenting with these different ways of providing information. Some of the experiments have worked better than others, and a lot of lessons have been learnt.

Actually, this is one of the main reasons why CD-ROM is suddenly becoming really popular. Two years ago, many CD-ROM discs really did look experimental. But with the experience gained from their experiments, software publishers have slowly been able to increase the quality and effectiveness of their multimedia publications, and it's only in the last year or two that truly excellent CD-ROM multimedia discs have started to reach the market.

'Interactivity' – the intangible aspect of multimedia

Most of the elements that go to make up a multimedia application are concrete and tangible, even though they are just different types of data – text, pictures, video and all the rest. There's one aspect, though, that you can't identify so easily, and yet it's probably the most important – and that's what we've come to call 'interactivity'.

Multimedia is very good at finding different ways of presenting information to you. But it also has to be good at helping you gain access to the information you want, and that's where the interaction comes in.

A CD-ROM application is interactive basically because you make decisions about what happens next. In an adventure game the interaction could be something quite simple, like deciding to travel north or giving the right answer to a puzzle - and the computer's response to your action. In an action game like a flight simulator, it's a more complex thing because your decisions – which way to fly, or whether to fire a missile – are being made constantly, and checked for by the computer many times a second.

A CD-ROM reference application like an encyclopedia requires a completely different kind of interaction. You must be able to choose from not just several possibilities, as in an adventure game, but thousands of possibilities. It must be easy for you to find a specific thing that you're looking for, but it must also be fun for you to browse around and see what you come across.

So the demands of multimedia interaction are pretty high. A successful CD-ROM disc will not only offer interesting and enjoyable content, but will also offer effective ways of enabling you to interact with the content.

Your primary means of interacting with a multimedia application will be the mouse: your secondary means will be the keyboard. So for the most part you'll find yourself clicking on areas of the screen with the mouse: selecting items from menus or lists of options, activating icons, clicking 'buttons'. From time to time you might type something in, such as a word for the application to search for in the text.

The basics of multimedia interaction

The basic principle of on-screen presentation of information in a multimedia CD-ROM application is very simple. When you start up the application you are presented with a screen that offers you a numbers of choices. You are able to select any of these choices by clicking with the mouse: when you do so, a window might open or a whole new 'screen' will appear with a new range of options for you to choose from.

So the basic form of multimedia is clicking through a number of screens. These screens are often called 'pages', by analogy with traditional books.

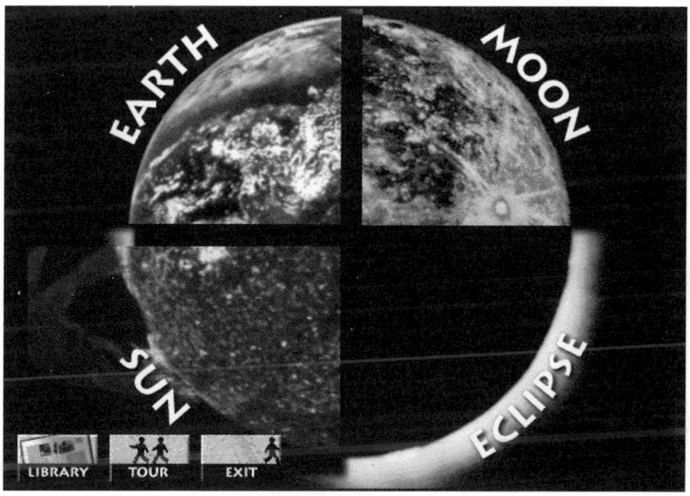

A very simple form of multimedia as seen in A View from Earth, an interactive CD-ROM book about the solar system. Click on one of the four main subjects and you're off to that 'chapter', which will give you another screen offering other choices.

Common conventions used in multimedia interaction

Experience over the last few years has helped publishers refine the methods of interaction that work best, and as a result there are certain 'conventions' that have grown up. Many of them are best described using the analogy of 'navigating' along a 'path' of information, with the choices you are offered on each screen being seen almost as side-turnings. Anyway, here are a few of the more important conventions.

'Smart' lists

With a reference work like an encyclopedia, no matter how sophisticated the presentation may be, the most practical and quickest way to find a subject you want is to look it up in a humble alphabetical list. 'Smart' lists have a space for you to type into, and as you type each new letter, the list jumps to the point in the list that where words that begin with those letters are found. So by the time you've typed 'bog', you might well have narrowed the choice to Bogart, Humphrey; Bogarde, Dirk; and places where peat is dug. Easy. All you have to do now is select the article you want, with the mouse, and it's displayed for you.

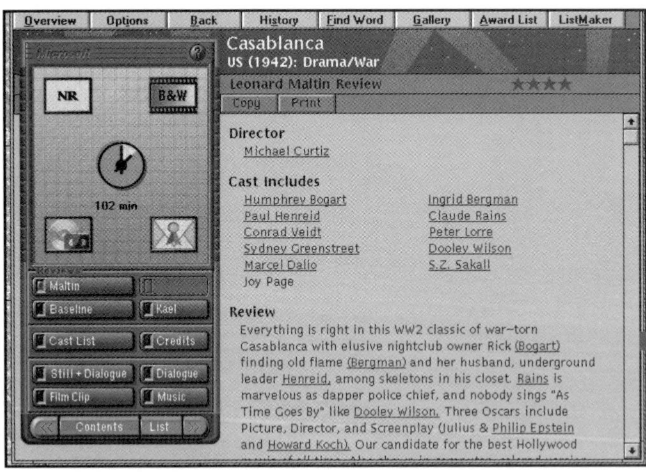

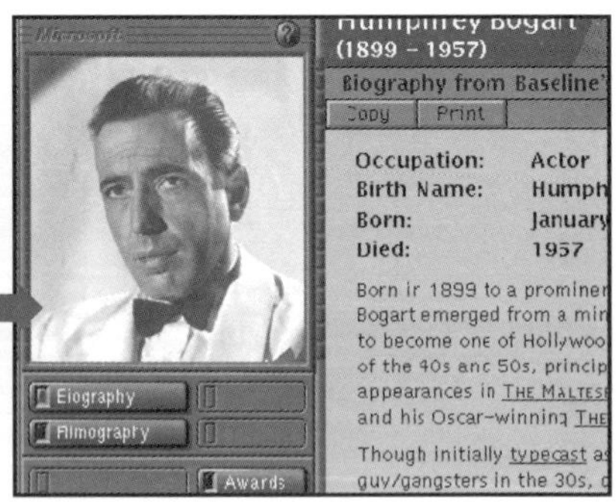

Hypertext in Cinemania – clicking on any of the highlighted words will immediately open an article on that subject.

Hypertext

Probably the single most unique feature of CD-ROM multimedia, in reference works especially. As you read the text of an 'article', you will notice certain words are in bold, or coloured. Clicking or double-clicking on one of these words will make another article appear on the screen; an article which is about the hypertext word you've selected.

Related topic menus

Not necessarily an either/or alternative to hypertext, a Related Topic menu is a list of other articles or entries in a reference work that are on a similar subject to an article that is currently displayed on the screen: any of the related topics can be called up with a click of the mouse, the idea being that it is easy to find material that is related to the topic you are currently viewing.

Go back

Invariably a situation will crop up where you 'take a wrong turn' as you 'navigate' through the information in a multimedia application, or reach a 'dead end', and so a Go Back button will return you to the previous screen that you were viewing. It's almost always one of the most important and most-used options.

'Home' button

Like the Go Back, except that this icon returns you to the main options screen of the application.

History

Since you can leap from topic to topic easily in most multimedia applications, the 'paths' by which you 'navigate' through the information can be quite complex. To help you go back to something you remember seeing earlier in a session, you often have the choice of pulling up a list of all the screens or articles that you have visited during a session, and you can return to a screen by clicking on its name in the History list. A History is also rather a fun thing, since you can see where a train of thought has taken you.

On-line dictionary

In some applications, the Hypertext option is replaced by a dictionary, where double-clicking on a word will bring up a window with a dictionary definition of that word.

Find word

Enables you to search for occurrences of any word (or, sometimes, set of words) within the entire text of a CD-ROM. Results are usually presented as a menu of article titles, so that you can see where your word crops up, and you select an item from the menu to view the article. Often you will also see a number displayed which shows how many occurrences of your word have been found. Often, too, your word will be highlighted wherever it occurs in the text.

Complex or filtered searches

As well as a simple search to find a word, you can usually access more complex searches. Some searches enable you to set specific limits for the search using options from a menu of search criteria: a good example of this would be the search screen in Microsoft's Cinemania, where you can filter out the films that share a particular star, or are of the same type (action, comedy etc) or have a high rating from the critics. Other searches allow you to search for a string of words, often connected using the Boolean operators AND, OR and NOT: so you might search an encyclopedia for articles that contain the words "ear AND nose AND throat" together, or items that contains the words "car OR van but NOT lorry".

Topic or chapter menus

Articles, pages or screens of information are often grouped together and organised into chapters of related items. These chapters might also be referred to as sections, topic groups, subject groups, categories or all sorts of other things, and they might also be sub-divided into smaller sections. The point in each case is that you can easily access a list of items that are related by subject, usually using a menu, as opposed to just using a simple or 'smart' list that contains all the articles on the disc.

Media galleries

Since one of the main advantages a multimedia disc like an encyclopedia has over a normal printed edition is its lavish use of pictures, sounds and video clips, it's quite common for you to be able to pick out the fun bits from Gallery lists of these media. Microsoft's Cinemania, for example, has Galleries of Stills and Portraits, Dialogue extracts, Music extracts and Videos.

Visual analogies

It's often more immediate to present information in a graphical form rather than as a list of words, so multimedia discs make extensive use of interactive graphical items which use real-world analogies to help

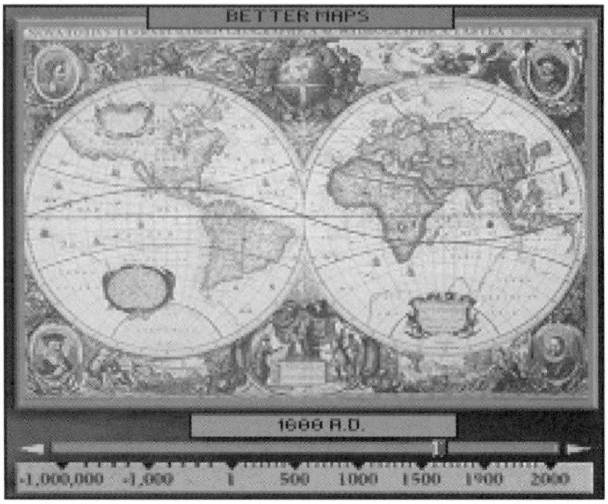

The use of a timeline can be very appropriate in multimedia, as with The Discoverers, a disc about various types of discovery and exploration through history. Timelines are also well used in biographical discs, and anything even vaguely historical can make good use of them.

you get the idea. So, for example, the coffee-table book about a journey across Australia, *From Alice to Ocean*, enables you to choose a chapter by clicking on any point on a map of the journey.

Many other discs also use maps and atlases to help you pinpoint subjects of interest, but other visual analogies are common too – using a bookshelf to select an item to read, for instance, or selecting a video clip by pressing the channel buttons on a TV.

Timelines

Another way of presenting information choices in an easy, visual, diagrammatic manner, the Timeline has become widely used. Essentially, it's just a chronological display, with a line on the screen showing the progress of the years; items that you can select are marked on the line at the appropriate point in history. Timelines are especially useful in reference works.

Typical multimedia applications

So what can be done with multimedia? Well, you must already have a vague idea, even if it's just that multimedia encyclopedias are big news at the moment. You might also know that many traditional print publishers, from Penguin to Time Warner, are experimenting with multimedia.

However, one of the most interesting things about multimedia is that it is already becoming very obvious that it works especially well for dealing with certain very specific types of material. Here's a brief look at some of the areas in which multimedia has shown great promise. All of these areas are already represented by excellent applications that you can buy as soon as you get your hands on a CD-ROM drive.

Reference books

A key fact about CD-ROM is its ability to store, and rapidly search through, large amounts of information. A dictionary is an obvious use

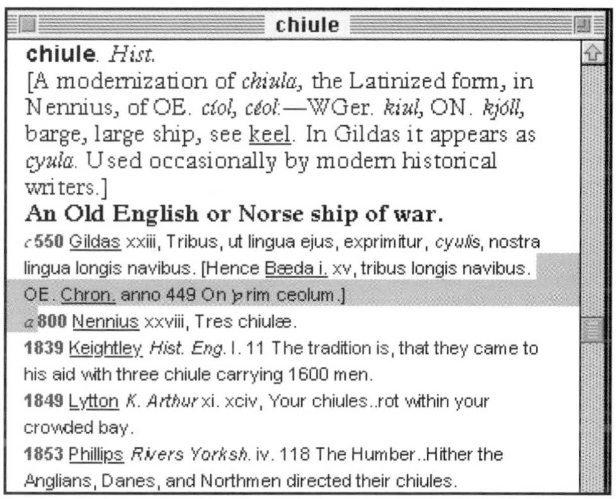
chiule

chiule. *Hist.*
[A modernization of *chiula*, the Latinized form, in Nennius, of OE. *cíol, céol*:—WGer. *kiul*, ON. *kjóll*, barge, large ship, see keel. In Gildas it appears as *cyula*. Used occasionally by modern historical writers.]
An Old English or Norse ship of war.
c **550** Gildas xxiii, Tribus, ut lingua ejus, exprimitur, *cyulis*, nostra lingua longis navibus. [Hence Bæda i. xv, tribus longis navibus. OE. Chron. anno 449 On þrim ceolum.]
a **800** Nennius xxviii, Tres chiulæ.
1839 Keightley *Hist. Eng.* I. 11 The tradition is, that they came to his aid with three chiule carrying 1600 men.
1849 Lytton *K. Arthur* xi. xciv, Your chiules..rot within your crowded bay.
1853 Phillips *Rivers Yorksh.* iv. 118 The Humber..Hither the Anglians, Danes, and Northmen directed their chiules.

The Oxford English Dictionary CD Edition offers pure reference, with 21 volumes of words and definitions.

for this power, with the added advantage that you can also use the computer to help you when you don't know how to spell a word.

However, multimedia is more than mere text. Even in a dictionary, you could add speech so the user can hear each word being pronounced, though such a dictionary has yet to appear. But the archetypal CD-ROM multimedia application is the encyclopedia, where animated diagrams, video clips, sound recordings, music and speech can all be used to bring the material to life.

There are lots of reference discs on specific subjects that apply the encyclopedia approach to a particular topic. The film guide Cinemania, for example, as well as lots of children's reference works. Other discs will use a different balance of material: for example atlases, which inevitably use the visual aspect (maps, photos and diagrams) far more than they use text.

Children's books

Certain types of multimedia seem to work much better than others, and there's a theory that this success is dependent on what your

From Broderbund's Living Books series, Ruff's Bone is a great example of an interactive children's book. you explore screens like this one, literally litered with objects, by clicking on the different elements of the picture to see what happens. Unlike in a reference work, your access to the material is unstructured and explorative, rather than purposeful.

'motive' is for interacting. Reference works like encyclopedias, for example, are very successful because you have a strong and immediate motive for interacting – you want to find something out. This makes it pretty easy for the publishers of an encyclopedia to come up with successful forms of interaction that help you find out what you want to know quickly and easily.

At the other end of the spectrum as far as motive for interacting goes, but equally successful, are children's interactive storybooks. These have attractive, animated picture-screens which a child clicks on to set off different events, such as more animations and sound effects. There is no immediate motivation, other than discovery, and so the interaction is a completely random browsing. You just click all over the screen, and see what happens.

Interactive children's books such as the Living Books series and the amazing TuneLand are immediately appealing to both kids and adults, they are almost like interactive cartoons. But much of their success, in my opinion, like reference works, is down to this motive business. In many situations, you need much more of a motive to explore a disc: in this case, random browsing is all you need.

Educational discs

There are plenty of educational and children's discs that fall into the category of reference, but there are others that use slightly different approaches. These tend to be a more 'useful' way of presenting the information than would be possible with any other sort of media, for reasons that relate to the use of the computer.

For example, many educational discs offer large resources of materials – photographs and text – which can be searched through, saved out and used in project work. No other medium than CD-ROM could offer this kind of resource.

Another typical form of educational CD-ROM is one that presents lessons in a structured form, and then enables a student to respond to them. Here the advantages are initially the mixed media – animations, videos and pictures all liven up the lessons in a way the teacher could only if he or she had a wide range of AV resources available, while a mixture of text and speech is especially useful for language lessons.

A second advantage is that the student can proceed at his or her own pace, while a third benefit is that the interactive nature of CD-ROM can be used for tests and quizzes which reinforce the learning process. Multimedia discs have great potential for making learning more interesting at home and in schools, and at all levels from primary schools to adult education.

Non-fiction books

This is a widely popular form of CD-ROM publication, but to date remains a largely unsuccessful one. The idea, simply enough, is to present a book-like publication, generally with screens of pictures

The non-fiction book is a popular choice for publishers wishing to experiment with multimedia. But this example – the coffee-table book From Alice to Ocean – points up some weaknesses. Screens like this, where you watch the photos and listen to a narration, are linear and not interactive.

accompanied by a narrated soundtrack replacing traditional pages of text and pictures.

The problem, of course, is that the narrative tends to be linear – the best way to read a book is to start at page one and go steadily through to the end – and the interaction tends to be limited to clicking on an icon to go to the next page. For a little added variety 'sidebars' or 'panels' with extra information might pop up occasionally, or you might be able to select specific chapters or sections from an interesting graphical menu such as a map; but these slight distractions from the main theme hardly add to the interactivity.

There are better examples, but these tend to be books which don't have a linear narrative in the first place, and they move towards the more successful multimedia form used by reference works.

Entertainment

Fiction, movies and music have all found new interactive forms on CD-ROM. The first two are represented by games, which can

Peter Gabriel's Xplora 1 – interactive pop music with video, and you can even sing along.

happily be viewed either as the interactive form of fictional writing, or as interactive films, depending on your point of view.

Interactive music is proving slightly more diverse and experimental because it's a much newer field than games, but like music in the real world it tends to split easily into classical and pop music.

The strongest use of multimedia in classical music is to provide on-screen notes that accompany a CD-DA hi-fi quality score as it plays. In this way, the classical enthusiast is able to learn to appreciate the music much more deeply, as well as being able to flick through background material like biographies and histories.

Interactive pop music is still finding its feet. In early efforts by Peter Gabriel, David Bowie and Prince, the CD-ROM is used as a multimedia platform to deliver music, videos, photos and speech (interviews with the artist, for instance) but all this is nothing new – a book and a video could do the same. The future of interactive music is likely to be as an artistic medium for creating virtual worlds, but we'll go into this in more detail in the chapter on entertainment.

Video in multimedia

Text, pictures, animation and digital sound are common features of all kinds of computer applications, but video is rather a different thing: it's pretty much exclusive to CD-ROM. Here's a quick run-through of what you need to know about it.

Video formats

There are two common forms of video used in CD-ROM applications – Microsoft's Video for Windows, which is used exclusively on the PC, and Apple's QuickTime, which is mostly for the Macintosh but can also be used on Windows PCs.

What are Video for Windows and QuickTime?

WHAT DOES IT MEAN?

Both Video for Windows and QuickTime are standard software systems which incorporate several different elements.

For starters, they establish standard file formats for the storage and interpretation of video clips, which equate to graphics file (things like PCX, GIF and PICT) or sound file formats. In other words, they ensure that lots of different makes of animation and video-producing software will all produce similar video files, no matter who publishes the software. Incidentally, many other kinds of software, such as WP and DTP packages, are developing the ability to use video clips, so that you can do things like add video memos to word-processed documents.

Most importantly, Video for Windows and QuickTime establish standard compression methods for compressed video with interleaved audio. As you know, a video sequence is composed of a number of frames (different pictures, in other words) which are brought to the screen in succession. Television uses 25 such frames every second.

In the tube. This is Video For Windows running on a 640-by-480 resolution Windows screen. (Shot taken from Maniac Sports.)

And this is a video of Country Joe Macdonald at Woodstock running in QuickTime on a Macintosh.

Video for Windows and QuickTime videos use a lower numbers of frames per second (fps or 'frame rate'), typically 12 to 15 fps, but all the same all these different images add up to a lot of data. Since a double-speed drive can only transfer 300K every second, the amount of data in each frame must be reduced by the compression methods, which do things like cutting out any data that remains the same from one image to the next.

Finally, as well as file formats and compression methods, both Video for Windows and QuickTime establish standards by which software can interact with hardware, such as a capture card which is used for digitising video footage onto the computer.

Limitations of video

Because of the limitations on data transfer rate, even after the compression techniques are used to squeeze extra data in, video clips are severely limited in the amount of data they can use for each frame. As a consequence, the size of the video window on your screen is severely limited – typically much less than a quarter of the screen – and increasing the size will only reduce the resolution so that the picture becomes 'blocky'. The number of colours used is also limited, usually to only 256. Video clips also require a lot of RAM – 4Mb is needed and 8Mb is better, on either Mac or PC.

What you need so that you can play videos

Both Video for Windows and QuickTime are software-only systems, so to play discs that use video clips you only need to add a little bit of extra software. Fortunately, this isn't something you need to buy – the small extension that you need is simply a run-time player program, and in both cases the run-time player is distributable with the permission of the copyright holder and is commonly included on the disc with CD-ROM applications that need them.

QuickTime: the QuickTime system extension is included on a separate floppy disk with System 7.1 or later. It also comes with most CD-ROM drive set-up software, as well as with applications that need it. To install it, you simply have to drag the QuickTime icon on to your closed System folder.

Video for Windows: files produced by VfW are known as AVI files (audio/video interleaved) and are usually distinguished by the .AVI extension on the filename. The Microsoft Windows MediaPlayer program can play these files, and the run-time VfW player is included with most new systems and with CD-ROM driver software as well as with applications that need it. It's generally installed by running a program called SETUP.EXE in a VFW directory.

New versions of Video for Windows and QuickTime

In 1994 new versions of both video formats were launched, with improved software compression bringing the ability to use larger-sized video windows on the screen.

Top Gun is seen here running on a PC screen from a Video CD disc.

Video for Windows 1.1 is an application intended for use by anyone who wants to create videos (in other words, you don't need to buy it if you only want to play videos that are provided on discs). This new version can produce videos up to 320 by 240 pixels at frame rates of up to 30 fps. The package includes various sound- and picture-editing tools as well as special effects transitions and a choice of new file-compression systems.

QuickTime 2 matches Video for Windows 1.1 with its ability to display sizes of 320 by 240 pixels running at frame rates of up to 30 fps, though it needs a 68040-based Mac to work properly. It's said that the new QuickTime will run at full-screen and full motion on a PowerMac, though it does this by doubling the pixel size, so it looks blocky close up. It also adds a timecode, to help with editing, and support for the Macintosh Music Architecture, which means music can be composed using a MIDI-style sequencer and played concurrently with the video – this avoids using sampled music and so cuts file sizes enormously.

Video CD

However good the recent developments in software compression, systems like Video for Windows and QuickTime will never be able to deliver what's known as 'full-screen, full-motion video', or 'FMV' for short: pictures that fill the screen at full resolution comparable at least to the 512 lines of PAL TV, run at the TV rate of 25fps, and have a full range of colours (at least 16-bit and preferably 14-bit). It can't be done.

There is a way that it can be done, however, and that's using hardware compression, where a set of chips is used to squeeze the data down during the production process, and then decompress it again when it reaches the computer after being read from the CD.

The Video CD standard uses this hardware compression method. It involves a set of chips which you fit on a card costing £2-300 inside your Mac or PC. The Video CD standard and its uses are explained in detail in a separate chapter.

Chapter 8
For the kids...

- Computers in schools
- Interactive fun and learning
- 'Edutainment'

TuneLand – pure entertainment for kids, but there are lots of CD-ROM titles that mix fun with learning, and others that are seriously educational.

Introduction

We haven't called this chapter 'education' for two reasons: children's software doesn't just mean education, and education doesn't just mean for children. There's a wide range of educational resources and reference titles which are aimed at older children, colleges, universities (for use by researchers as well as students) and adult education.

At the same time, there are a good many CD-ROM titles for younger children which are designed primarily as a form of entertainment, not to teach – and yet even these may offer quite substantial educational benefits, in much the same way that any book will encourage and improve reading skills, even if it's not a learn-to-read book.

During this chapter we'll take a look at the sort of CD-ROM titles that are available for children from pre-school to secondary school level, and at the sorts of benefits the discs might have over traditional forms of teaching.

Little Monster at School from the Living Books series. Is it learning, or just for fun?

Computers in schools

Since the early 1980s computers have played a key part in education in British schools. Their importance as future tools of everyday work was recognised early by the Department of Education, and initiatives to put computers in all primary schools – which selected the BBC Model B as the standard equipment – have proved pretty effective.

The most important development was a vast change from the early days of computers in schools – it was quickly realised that having separate Computer Studies courses, or studying the inner workings of the machines in maths and physics classes, was not the correct way forward. Instead, the use of computers was integrated into the everyday classroom environment. So how are computers used in schools?

Computers in primary schools

In primary schools one of the main aims is simply familiarisation, so that children don't have the fear of computers that afflicts the older generation. After that, one of the main uses is with a simple programming language called Logo, which uses geometrical methods to draw shapes on the screen. This teaches logic as well as simple maths, algebra and geometry. It sounds complex, but it's amazing how quickly children take to it, and they're using it in intake year, at the age of four or five.

Following that, the most popular programs in primary schools are adventure games. Not the sort that you might buy purely for leisure use, but special educational ones where the problems that have to be solved are mathematical or linguistic. These problems reinforce the teaching of maths and reading, but more importantly, they develop problem-solving skills per se. Also, because sessions at the computer are shared among small groups of children, each problem can be used to encourage discussion, cooperation, and shared problem-solving. All of these are important social, as well as intellectual, skills.

Computers in secondary schools

Secondary schools are most likely to be using powerful machines such as Apple Macs and PCs to run exactly the same sort of software that is used in offices and businesses across the country – word processing, databases, spreadsheets, DTP, graphics and so forth.

The idea is that the use of computers can be integrated into everyday subjects in just the same way that it is in the wider world of work. In art or design classes, for example, illustration and DTP programs can be used instead of traditional paint or ink, just as they are by professional illustrators and designers. Why shouldn't a project for English, history or geography be presented with a word processor or a DTP program? Why not use a spreadsheet to record and analyse the results of experiments in physics or chemistry?

So in the secondary school context, a computer plus the right software is mostly used as a tool, just the way it is in real life. However, with specific software, the computer also has a role as another weapon in the armoury of A/V (audio-visual) aids, so children can be left to work through a program that's just as interesting as a video or a film would be, and possibly more useful.

Battle of the sexes

One thing that is very much worth watching for if you're a parent is the proven tendency of boys to dominate use of a computer in a situation where both sexes have access. It's not that girls are any less capable with the technology or any less keen to use it, but experience of teachers in the classroom shows that boys tend to be more pushy, and girls tend to be more willing to stand back and let someone else take over. If you're not careful, the boys can tend to get more than their fair share of time on the computer. Bear it in mind.

The government and CD-ROM

The UK Government has seen the value of CD-ROM for educational purposes and has put its money where its mouth is, encouraging the use of CD-ROM systems in the classroom and also contributing to the development of what it sees as appropriate CD-ROM software.

A 1993 initiative saw two-thirds of Britain's secondary schools, some 23,000, being equipped with CD-ROM hardware, and a further initiative by the Department for Education in 1994 set aside £4.5 million to ensure that a substantial proportion of Britain's primary schools would also be supplied with CD-ROM hardware and software.

Equally importantly, £700,000 was invested in the development of 12 specific CD-ROM titles, all of which would support the teaching of subjects within the National Curriculum.

CD-ROM for pre-school

There's no reason why children should not be allowed, indeed encouraged, to use the computer as soon as they are old enough to hold and use the mouse. In fact, there are special mice available which are more suited to younger hands, with smaller bodies and bigger buttons, and these can be a worthwhile investment. How young should they start? Well, the educational sales manager for a large computer firm once told me that his kids of two and three were very keen on 'splashing around' with a computer paint package.

Ideally, a good CD-ROM application for younger children should only need a parent to start up the software: the kids should then be able to get on with it themselves, requiring only the interaction of clicking around the screen with the mouse. Naturally enough, the keyboard is of limited use if you haven't yet learnt to read.

Interactive storybooks

There are many good CD-ROM interactive children's books which would be ideal for pre-school as well as for primary school children. Good examples are the discs in the Living Books series from Broderbund, which are distributed in the UK by Electronic Arts. Demo versions of the first four titles in the series have cropped up on the cover-mounted CDs of many a magazine, as well as being available on a mini-CD from the publishers, so you should be able to track them down and try them before buying.

Familiar names from children's books are cropping up with increasing frequency on CD-ROM, with Dr Seuss recently signed up for a

Ruff's Bone, another Living Book, fun for kids and adults alike.

Wiggins in Storyland actually lets children create their own settings and make up stories to go with them. It's proving quite popular.

Living Books appearance and Richard Scarry's creations making an appearance for Time Warner.

Like all books, interactive storybooks on CD-ROM have words: so reading will be developed in children who can already read. The words are not, however, necessary, since narration is added in digital audio form. Reading aloud to your children can be hard work: with CD-ROM, that hard work is done for you.

Generally, each 'page' of the book is represented by a single screen in the CD-ROM title, and the text of each page will be highlighted as the narration proceeds. Often, children can also move the mouse pointer over individual words in the text and click on them to hear them read out, which encourages youngsters who are just starting to read, and helps to develop vocabulary in children who are already reading.

The entertainment part of these interactive books is usually provided by animation and sound effects, and the interaction comes at the end of each screen when the child can explore the pictures, clicking on characters and pieces of scenery to make things happen, and so triggering animations, sounds and all manner of fun things.

These kinds of kids' books are one of the most successful types of CD-ROM application yet to appear. If you have young children, you can't go far wrong.

Puzzles and games

The other common type of disc for younger children is collections of puzzles and games. As you might expect, the puzzles themselves often have an educational leaning. When they get beyond the obvious number puzzles and spelling tests the purpose of the games can often be a little more obscure, but the games themselves are generally more imaginative and rewarding.

Usually, the main benefit that is added by the use of CD-ROM instead of a traditional floppy disk medium is not to enhance the games themselves, but to add lots of extra sounds, voices and animation which make the whole thing much more fun that it would otherwise be.

Putt-Putt goes to the Moon from Hormungous Entertainment is a typical puzzles and games children's disc, and fun to boot.

Sometimes the puzzles on a disc of this type are seemingly pretty trivial – things like noughts and crosses, spelling tests and match-the-pairs games are all very obvious and soon become less than interesting, even though educationalists do say these kinds of simple logic puzzles are beneficial. More interesting are other variations, the more original the better, and there is now a wide choice of adventure-type games which are particularly good.

Dinosaurs and rocket ships...

It's time for that never-popular segment of our programme, 'Memories of an ageing computer journalist'. When I was a kid, I well remember that one of my favourite books was an encyclopedia of aircraft, lavishly illustrated with superb drawings and paintings. It was actually aimed at much older readers than I was when I first got it, but I recall that it remained a favourite of mine for years, only growing in interest when I was old enough to read the full text.

Aircraft are still popular with children, as are cars, spaceships, dinosaurs, bug-eyed insects and all kinds of other strange things. One

Grolier's Prehistoria featured dinosaurs but proved there was more to prehistoric life than reptiles.

of the most popular types of CD-ROM disc is a variant of the adult reference works at which CD-ROM has excelled. The children's encyclopedia, knowledge adventure book or treasury – call it what you will – uses similar techniques to the adult reference works to present encyclopedic quantities of information in an attractive and entertaining way.

Science topics predominate, and there are certain subjects which are especially popular – the kind of things that children through the years have always loved. Especially boys, it has to be said – as ever with computers, the CD-ROM software seems to be slanted in favour of the kind of activities that females are encouraged to steer clear of. At the last count there were six or seven different CD-ROMs about dinosaurs, for instance, and that's not including games. Space exploration is another very popular one.

What's 'edutainment'?

Beyond the sort of things that kids are obsessed with anyway, there are also plenty of other discs which might be just as popular in the classroom or in the home. An example would be Microsoft's Ancient Lands, a survey of life in ancient Rome, Greece and Egypt. By the standards of the classroom it's great fun, but by the standards of having fun it's a little scholarly. There are plenty of discs that cross the borders in this way, and that's partly why the label 'edutainment' has grown up to describe the blend of entertainment with education.

Children's reference

As well as discs on specific topics like space, dinosaurs or ancient history, there are more general reference works such as children's encyclopedias of science. In this book we're trying not to refer too heavily to individual titles, though it's difficult not to use specific

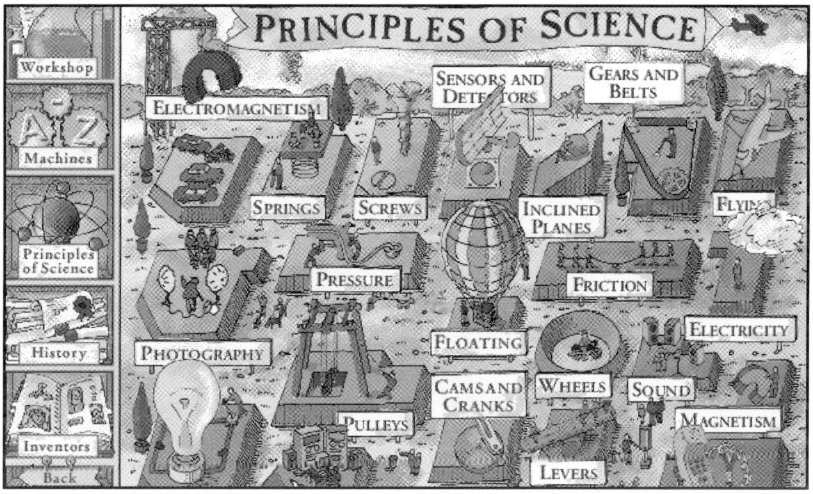

Dorling Kindersley's Eyewitness Encyclopedia of Science – a leader among children's reference multimedia titles.

examples on occasion, but we really do have to mention Dorling Kindersley's range of discs in the children's reference genre.

DK are the ideal example because they already publish many books of this kind using the traditional medium of ink on paper. Their first experience with multimedia was in collaboration with Microsoft on the Musical Instruments title, which used the typical DK approach of lavish illustration but added multimedia elements like the ability to hear every instrument being played.

DK's new-for-1994 range of independently-published discs builds on this approach by adding lots of animation to the already strong visuals. Their discs cover subjects such as the human body, 'how things work' and and encyclopedia of science.

I wouldn't want to give the impression that DK's are the only discs of this kind available, however. There's a wide range of reference works that take a slightly different slant from similar adult-oriented titles.

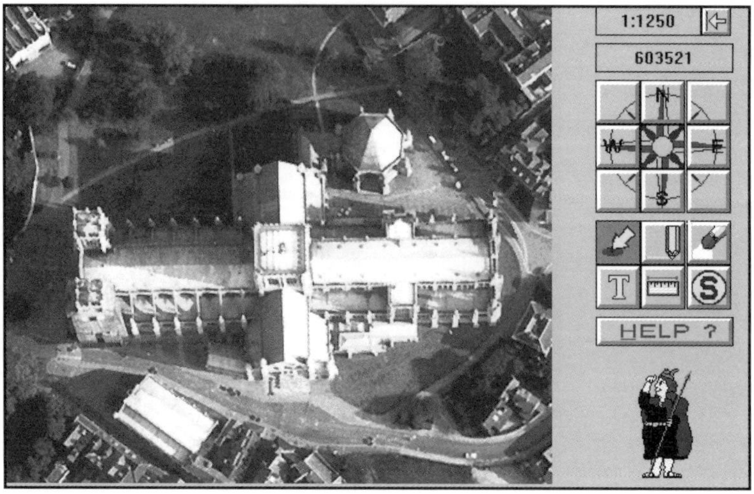

Linked to the National Curriculum, Discover York teaches geography. It is a little too serious, but could titles like this could still cross over to the home market as well.

Strictly for schools

There are many CD-ROM titles that are probably a little too serious to be taken on by parents in the home. Very often, these discs are superb ways of teaching specific subjects, especially science subjects such as chemistry, but they tend to need the support work of extensive teacher's notes, and to need close involvement and support from a teacher.

So that's a little warning, but it doesn't mean that these discs need not be bought for home use. Invariably, the multimedia element is used to make what could be rather dull, dry subjects into vastly more entertaining ones, with the extensive use of video, animation and so on to liven it all up.

Very often, the main teaching method used by these discs is exploration followed by testing. Now the idea of 'tests' might sound dull, but thanks to the huge popularity of trivia board games and TV quizzes, almost everyone likes a good quiz. And in most cases, the testing element of these discs comes over much more like a quiz than a test. It's rather fun to try the tests at the start, to see how little you know.

Tests have the great benefit of helping the student to monitor his or her own progress without the teacher's involvement, but they're not the only benefit of the interactive nature of a CD-ROM title. The other great thing is that the student can explore at his or her own pace, and choose which bits to cover at any particular time. For this latter purpose, some sort of system that monitors which topics have been covered is a useful and helpful addition.

These three benefits of interaction – testing to monitor progress, being able to go at any pace, and being able to choose what order to cover things in – add to the experience. Interaction apart, though, the main advantage of CD-ROM titles is that they replace all kinds of other A/V material. Animations, video and sound are all much more accessible than static books, but the only way to get them normally is with videos and films, which may well be inconvenient as well as offering no individual control over the pace at which information is imparted.

What's adult, then?

Finally, it's worth mentioning that many of the 'adult' reference works – and we don't mean pornographic – may be just as accessible and useful to children, and especially older kids such as teenagers. Encyclopedias, dictionaries and atlases are all part of any good bookshelf and can equally well be staples of a CD-ROM library, and will all prove immensely useful when it comes to homework and projects.

Chapter 9
The CD-ROM Library

- Reference
- Languages
- Travel
- Computers
- Home and leisure
- Literature
- Popular non-fiction

Microsoft's Bookshelf is a rather literal interpretation of what this chapter's about. It's a collection of seven different reference books on one disc, including a dictionary, thesaurus, atlas and encyclopedia.

Introduction

There are so many different kinds of CD-ROM disc that it's difficult to know how to categorise many of them, but making the effort in spite of this, we though it would be useful to set aside a chapter of this book to cover all the different kinds of CD-ROM discs that are essentially multimedia forms of traditional, printed books. And there's a truly enormous range.

Encyclopedias, dictionaries and atlases are just the start. More or less anything that you might find in the non-fiction parts of a bookshop, from travel guides to cookery books, from car manuals to wildlife, is also represented on CD-ROM.

It's important to stress 'non-fiction', however. 'Interactive fiction' on CD-ROM has been tried a couple of times and has failed spectacularly, and there's a very good reason for that – it's been flourishing for years under the different guise of computer games. A good adventure game is a story that you can participate in, and hence both an interactive novel and an interactive movie.

Having said that, you can get the text of classic novels, poems and plays on CD-ROM. Anyway, let's browse through the CD-ROM bookshelf…

Reference section

Encyclopedias are the archetypal multimedia application, and there's a good choice of different ones available, but dictionaries and atlases are also popular too. If you're after a thesaurus or a crossword dictionary on CD-ROM, that can be tracked down without too much effort.

Reference works are ideally suited to CD-ROM for several reasons. Firstly, the medium is ideal for the storage of vast amounts of text, and makes it terrifically easy to search through that text for whatever you want. Secondly, the form of interaction – picking put one thing and letting the computer go off to search for it – is easy for a computer program to implement effectively. Thirdly, a multimedia disc can add pictures, sounds, music, animations and video to make it all more fun than the traditional printed book can handle.

Encyclopaedias

With speedy and flexible search systems, multimedia encyclopaedias make it quick and easy to look things up, even if you're not quite sure what you're looking for. This, together with their size – most CD-ROM publications represent printed equivalents of about 20 volumes – gives them immediate benefits over the printed editions before you even consider the added enhancements of video and sound.

We've already mentioned these enhancements a couple of times in this book, so to expand on the theme a little, here's a typical example of how a multimedia entry in an encyclopedia might work.

Imagine, for the sake of argument, that you look up the word 'car' in the encyclopedia. Assuming it's been properly Anglicised from an American original – and the fact that so many discs are of American origin remains one of the biggest stumbling blocks for CD-ROM in Britain – a whole choice of articles might now appear, perhaps with an introductory one on the general subject, and maybe even with an outline that summarises the introductory article and makes it easier to find the bit you want.

Bold words might indicate Hypertext links to other articles that will explain different aspects of the car. A 'further reading' or 'related topics' menu might also offer lots of other related articles. So there's plenty of material made easily accessible, but more importantly, there's lots of audio-visual material too.

There might be lovely 24-bit photos of vintage cars, for example, which you could perhaps save out to incorporate into some project of your own. So that you better understand how a car works, you might be able to watch an animation of a car engine, showing the complicated four-stroke cycle. You may be able to watch a video of Nigel Mansell winning the Formula One World Championship, perhaps.

Take other examples – look up Martin Luther King and you might see a portrait photo as well as being able to listen to an extract from his 'I have a dream' speech. Look up Louis Armstrong, and you could hear some of his music. Look up Chinese, and hear the Chinese language being spoken.

All these things make a multimedia encyclopedia great fun to use, and that in turn increases its usefulness, because you're much more likely to follow sidetracks (via the Hypertext and Related Topics menus) and find out much more than you would with a normal encyclopedia. Fun brings results.

We've already mentioned one big drawback of the first generation (1992-4) of encyclopedias, which is that they are mostly American in origin and so have rather different priorities from those of a British audience. The sports section will feature baseball heavily, for example, while 'soccer' barely gets a mention.

Hopefully one trend for the future will be that specifically British discs will become more common. Another trend could be encyclopedias that come on several discs – Microsoft's *Encarta* already has to use pretty sophisticated compression techniques to squeeze all its data on to one disc. One last thing that we may see more of is the use of animated diagrams, which could be invaluable for explaining technical subjects, like our car engine example above.

So there is a good deal of room for a much better multimedia encyclopedia on the market. However, no matter how much room for improvement you can find, and in spite if the fact that I'm not supposed to mentioning specific titles, Microsoft's *Encarta* already stands out as the best encyclopedia from the presentation point of view and is a worthy addition to any CD-ROM collection.

Dictionaries

'Practical' has so far won out over 'fun' when it comes to the implementation of CD-ROM dictionaries. The thing that's always seemed to me to be an ideal use for multimedia in a dictionary is having sound recordings so that you can hear pronunciations of difficult words, but it's an idea that has not yet seen the light of day except in an American edition (Websters) with about 3,500 pronunciations.

The CD-ROM dictionaries we've seen to date use the medium purely to store text, with no fancy additions. There is, however, one great advantage that the computer format has over a printed edition, and that's the fact that you can look up a word even if you can't spell it.

Using 'wild-card' characters like *, # or ? to mean 'an unknown letter goes here' or 'several unknown letters go here', you can look up words using just the bare bones of the spelling, and find out what the correct spelling should be.

Other advantages of the electronic form vary with the software. Some dictionaries have the ability to decode anagrams, some have the entries written out in full, doing away with those confusing abbreviations. You can generally search for a particular word in the entire text of the definitions, as well as just looking up 'headwords' the way you normally would in a dictionary. You might also be able to pick out particular types of word, such as foreign words.

In contrast to encyclopedias, one thing dictionaries on CD-ROM don't suffer from is a predominance of American editions. Several of the most popular English dictionaries are available, including the Collins, Chambers English and Oxford Concise. Oxford also publish their Thesaurus and Dictionary of Quotations as CD editions.

The peculiar thing about the compact dictionaries is that they actually only take up about 20Mb of data, and so it is often recommended that you install the entire thing to your hard drive, provided you have the space. This is not true, however, of the king of all dictionaries, the complete *Oxford English*, an etymological dictionary which is the standard reference for all academic language work and which in its printed form takes up 21 volumes.

The complete *OED* is an impressive beast, and comes in at the impressive price of £495. This might seem expensive, but the price has been carefully calculated so that libraries can acquire not only the disc, but also a complete multimedia PC, for roughly the same amount of money which would buy the £2,000 printed edition.

Atlases

There are quite a few CD-ROM atlases available nowadays, but they don't all have quite the approach that you might expect. They tend to be quite strong on facts and figures (populations, crops, exports, annual rainfall and the like) which might make them pretty useful for geography studies in a school environment, but they tend to be less strong on the actual maps.

Your average multimedia atlas will be happy, for example, to get no more detailed than a single-screen map showing the whole of the British Isles – though again, because they tend to be American in origin, they will usually show you each individual State of the USA. If you're lucky, you might be able to see physical (relief) maps as well as general, political or transport maps. Some atlases do, however, zoom in to greater levels of detail and even include street maps of the major cities of the world.

As ever, one advantage of multimedia is its ability to integrate pictures, sounds and video clips: so by clicking on London on the map of the UK, you might be able to see some of the capital's sights,

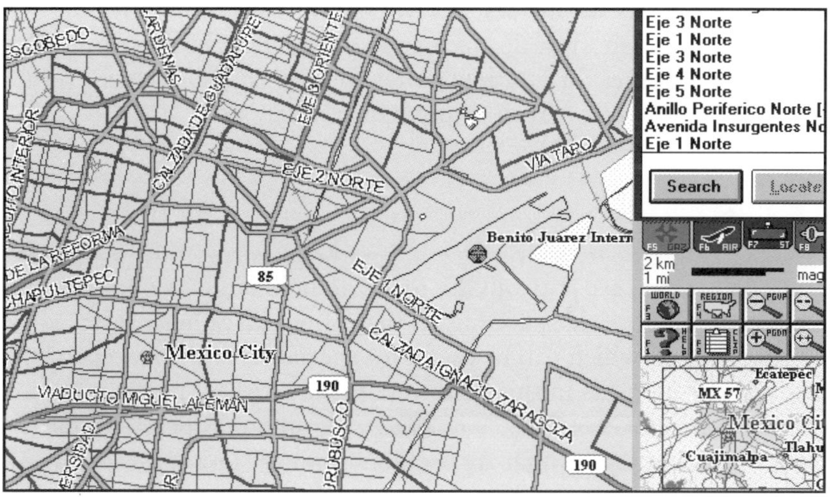

The Global Explorer Atlas can zoom right in as far as street maps for some of the world's major cities.

The Software Toolworks World Atlas has the more populist approach, with little detail but plenty of videos and photos.

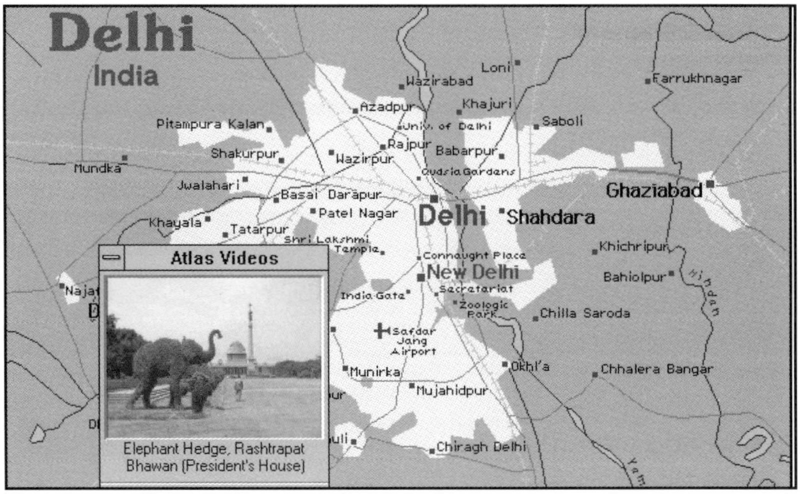

as well as perhaps listening to the national anthem. Some atlases concentrate mostly on the audio-visual approach and offer detailed photographic slideshow tours of the countries, as well as things like examples of the indigenous folk music, which can be highly entertaining as well as useful.

There is, incidentally, one prime example of a road atlas on CD-ROM, and that's *AutoRoute Plus*. It costs an enormous £595, but it's intended for use by businesses and will not only plan routes for maximum speed, shortest distance or greatest fuel efficiency, but will also work out routes for multiple visits. You can zoom in to see every single road in the UK, which is impressive stuff.

Resources

Using the storage capacity of CD-ROM to hold large amounts of text in a very small physical space means that firms can publish vast resources of text which can be useful for specialists and researchers. Probably the pioneers in this field were the broadsheet newspapers. *The Independent*, *Guardian*, *Times*, *Telegraph* all publish collections of a year's worth of text, which are useful not only to journalists but also to school and college libraries. Foreign newspapers, from *Le Monde* to the *Jewish Chronicle*, are also available.

There are all sorts of other things you can get on CD-ROM besides newspapers, though, some of which are quite surprising. The parliamentary record *Hansard* is available on CD, for instance. The *Times Educational Supplement* publishes a disc detailing half a million books, complete with reviews, while *Whitakers* publish a listing of 700,000 books. There is also a database of university and college courses, a record of legal developments and precedents since 1985 and a listing of 400,000 key UK companies.

Such resources seem likely to become even more commonplace to fulfil the specific needs of all kinds of professions and trades. Incidentally, British Telecom's CD-ROM database of all UK domestic and business telephone numbers is available for about £1,000. They have so far managed to fight off competition from a US firm which has been unable to publish its own version of the CD-ROM at only £50, because UK law assigns copyright in the data to BT.

One other trend worth mentioning is the increasing use of visual resources on CD-ROM, as well as textual ones. The famous Hulton picture library led the way in 1994, and it is more than likely that other photo libraries will follow suit, publishing collections of images using the Photo CD standard.

The foreign languages section

Foreign-language dictionaries are already available on CD-ROM, but not in any great quantity. There are, however, any number of teach-yourself language courses of all sorts of different approaches, aimed at all sorts of ages from young children to adults, and including specific titles aiming to teach language for use in business rather than on holiday.

Learn French with Asterix is one of those that will test your progress in writing and reading another language.

One obvious advantage of CD-ROM over other computer media is that it can hold proper CD-DA audio, so it can act just like a tape, video or Linguaphone record, giving you actual examples of the foreign language that you can listen to and repeat.

The advantage that CD-ROM has over, say, a video language lesson is that it is interactive: so you can go at your own pace, and repeat bits as often as you want. It can also test you as you go along and mark your work to see how well you scored, which a book can't do. In theory, a CD-ROM application could also monitor your progress and work out which your strengths and weaknesses are, then modify the lessons so that you work at your weak points, but as yet we've not seen this idea implemented in language discs.

Obviously, a computer application can monitor your written work because you'll type it in to the program, but it can't do anything about your spoken use of a new language. Several CD-ROM discs, however, which has come up with something of a solution to this problem.

The Learn French with Asterix series of discs has a fairly simple approach to expanding your spoken French, and is one example of this solution. You listen to an Asterix story being read in its native

You can get a taste of Japan with Berlitz for Business Japanese, a good example of a language-learning package aimed squarely at adults. This disc also has a feature that lets you record your own Japanese pronunciations and play them back. Then you'll hear just how to improve your spoken Japanese.

language, with the pictures displayed on the screen. It's actually quite useful as a reinforcement and for practice, though it won't actually teach you French.

The clever bit, though, is that the software includes a basic sound sampler, so that you can hook up a microphone to your Mac or to the sound card of your PC and record your own voice repeating the French words. When you play your version back alongside the original, it's surprising how noticeable your mistakes are, and it really does help you improve your pronunciation.

That's probably the most original use of a multimedia computer's capabilities which we've seen to date, but it doesn't necessarily make the series an outstanding one. There are all sorts of less enterprising titles which nevertheless teach language more effectively.

You can easily track down a beginner's course that will give you a good grounding in the obvious European languages like French, Spanish, Italian or German. Generally these discs take an approach which is closer to the teaching of language in schools, going for a full treatment that includes some aspects of the foreign culture. The equivalent of a phrasebook, intended specifically for holidaymakers who want to be able to get by in hotels and restaurants or on public transport, is not at all common. Only some language titles actually include written as well as spoken language, so this factor could help you choose.

Other languages besides the obvious are also available – Japanese, for example – and there is also a clump of titles that offer specific lessons for using a foreign language in business, rather than just in everyday situations.

The travel section

There's not yet an extensive range of travel guides available on CD-ROM, but there is quite a wide variety of different approaches among the handful of existing titles, and it does seem likely that this will be a major growth area in CD-ROM publishing over the next couple of years.

You can already get travel guides in the archetypal Baedeker's tradition, where an author picks out sights that are worth seeing and

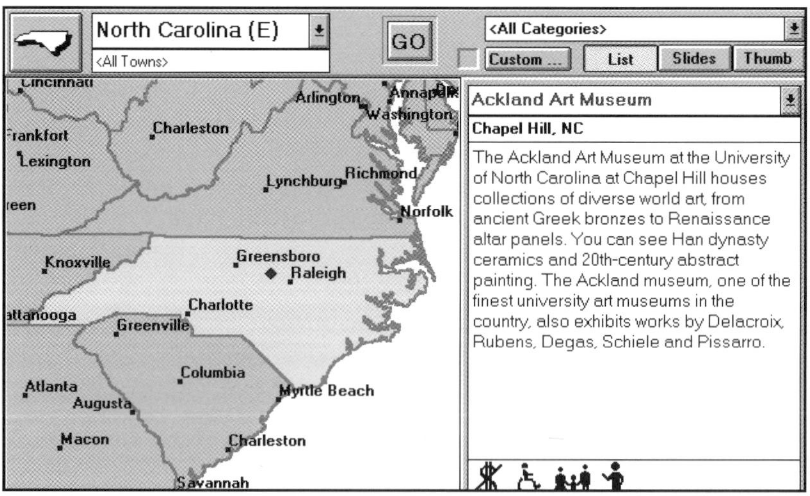

The Everywhere USA Travel Guide offers a practical and sensible approach to selecting tourist sights in the US.

France at its Best is a dull interpretation of a traditional guide book.

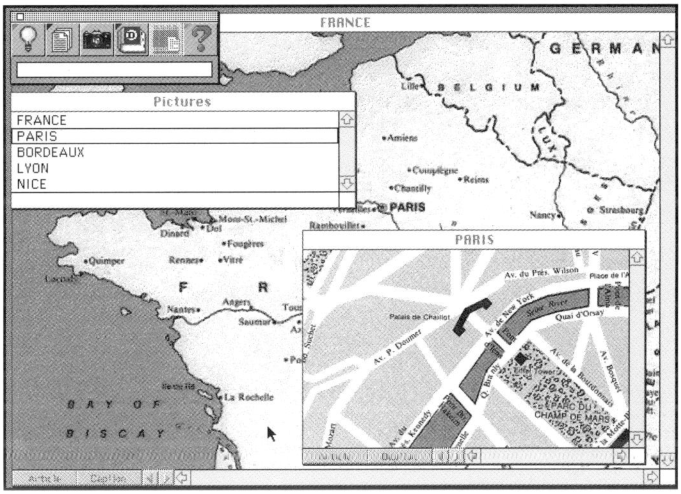

recommends hotels, restaurants and so on. Popular European destinations such as France, Spain and the UK are covered, though I have yet to see a disc that can compare with a good printed guidebook. And, after all, you can't take your PC with you when you're backpacking round Europe.

There are also colourful, glossy titles covering countries like Mexico and the USA which tend to look great, lavishly illustrated with both photos and video clips, and discs of this kind might help you decide on a destination in much the same way watching the Holiday programme on TV would – but these do tend to be short on practical information.

The most successful travel guides tend to be ones that are straightforward, actual guides to places to visit in a particular country, giving details like travel directions, opening times and so on. An excellent example is the *Everywhere USA Travel Guide*, which is simply a two-disc catalogue of places to go, including scenic sites such as national parks and man-made places such as museums. You can choose which State of the USA to visit and browse through the highlights of that State (all the locations are illustrated with photographs), then print out details. Hopefully more discs of this kind will soon become available.

The computer section

Not a large section of the CD-ROM library, this one, but one that's worth mentioning all the same. There are a couple of 'How it Works' titles, taking a multimedia approach to explaining computers, with lots of pictures, animations and videos. There are also a couple of collections of computer books that cram a whole bookshelf of books onto one disc, and though these are American in origin, they can be extremely useful for PC owners since they tend to cover a wide range of subjects relevant in the UK, from using popular programs such as specific makes of word processors and spreadsheets, to fitting CD-ROM drives.

Home and leisure

Cookery books and medical encyclopedias are pretty commonplace on CD-ROM, though as ever these do tend to be based on printed editions of popular American titles. There are even wine guides, baby books and interactive exercise videos to be had. Ooh, and there's a lovers' guide too, if you're feeling a bit saucy.

If pottering about in the garden is more your kind of thing, there are a number of gardening titles, from databases of plants that show what conditions the plants are suited for and help you pick out hardy perennials of the right colour, to dictionaries of plant diseases that will help you diagnose what's wrong with your wilting foliage and help to cure it.

You might prefer more passive pastimes, and if you're a film buff there are a variety of film guides on offer with Microsoft's outstanding *Cinemania* standing out from the crowd. *Cinemania* will not only help

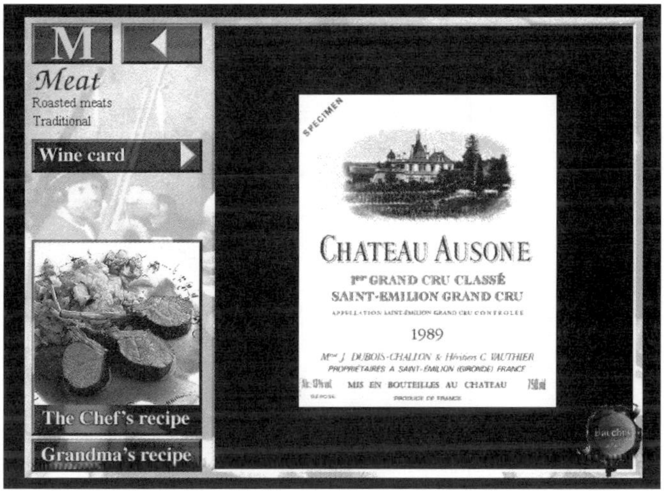

Select the right wine and recipe to match with the Bacchus and Comus gourmet guide.

you remember who starred in what, or pick out a movie to rent from the local video shop, but will also fill you in on cinematic techniques, give you a full biography of an actor or director and even play clips from films, extracts from the dialogue or bits of those famous movie soundtracks.

The visual arts are also well represented, with a wide range of titles covering everything from the Renaissance to Impressionism to modern photography. It seems likely that this leisure category is going to see an explosion in the number of titles available over the next few years.

The classical literature section

We've already said that interactive fiction is not really a viable idea because games are already filling that space, but that doesn't mean that you cant get fiction on CD-ROM. In particular, the storage capacity of CD is used for collections of classical texts. What exactly these can be used for is hard to say. Harper Collins, in their Ex Libris series, have published the collected works of Jane Austen and the Bronte sisters, but only their Lewis Carroll collection offers anything

Microsoft's Art Gallery offers a great way to learn to appreciate the paintings of the National Gallery.

more than the text of the books plus a search engine and the odd illustration. The Carroll disc features CD-DA extracts of Gielgud reading from *Alice in Wonderland*, but if you want that, you could buy a cassette tape.

Even though the collected writings of a particular author might set you back only £15, and a complete bookshelf of some of the world's most famous writing might be only £20, it's hard to see why anyone would want books in this form. You can't realistically expect to read them on the screen of a computer, and it's not economically viable to print them out (buying the book would be cheaper).

Possibly the only purpose for such computer editions of classical texts is for scholarly research, where being able to count the number of times the word 'blood' is used in Macbeth is the sort of thing people actually find useful.

In general, though, it seems these discs are on offer simply 'because it's there'. Because the texts have been entered into computers for academic research, they are widely available in the public domain, and especially on the academic networks. It's easy for shareware companies to gather together a number of these texts and sling them out on one disc. it's also very easy to be tempted into buying something that offers you the whole history of literature, from the *Egyptian Book of the Dead* to Dickens's greatest hits via the complete works of Shakespeare, all for only £20. But what would you do with it?

One justification for a CD-ROM edition is that it can be packaged into a complete educational format, with the addition of a structured series of study aids, comprehension tests and so on. Unfortunately, there are no good examples of this type of disc yet available. You can, incidentally, already buy collections of study aids (criticism and comment, such as Barron's notes) on CD-ROM, which might appeal to A-level students but should be beneath the notice of undergraduates.

There is, however, one outstanding example of the literature collection on CD-ROM, and that's the complete collection of English-language poetry, which costs many thousands of pounds but represents an astonishing academic resource.

Popular non-fiction

It's difficult to know how to describe this part of the CD-ROM library. It's all the sort of stuff you might find in the window, or on nice display shelves near the entrance of a bookshop – the kind of books that people buy as Christmas presents, translated into CD-ROM form.

There is, for instance the *Guinness Disc of Records*, which is a lot more entertaining than the printed edition because of its extensive use of videos and colour pictures, and the addition of a random browse facility that flicks through a slideshow of records from the disc. It's good fun, but it's hard to imagine anyone using it enough to justify the price.

The Guinness Disc of Records is actually far more fun than the book.

Coffee-table books have had a high profile in the early days of CD-ROM, with examples like Douglas Adams' *Last Chance to See*, and the Apple-developed tale of a woman's camel-back journey across Australia, *From Alice to Ocean*.

Alice to Ocean comes in a £50 package with a gorgeous printed edition of the book. But the CD-ROM part of the product, like the Douglas

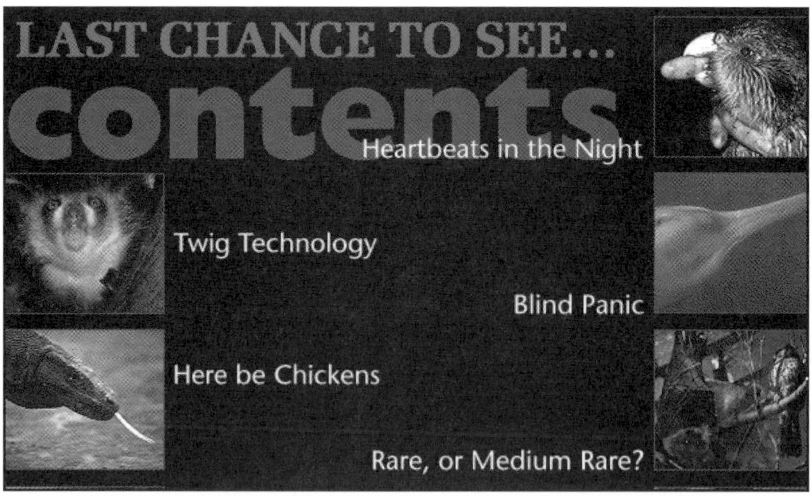

Douglas Adam's Last Chance to see is a super book, but it's not that great on CD-ROM.

Adams book, is disappointing. It's effectively only a slideshow of photos with narration (in the case of Last Chance to See the narration is actually by the author, but *From Alice to Ocean* is narrated by an actress). Both are very pretty and quite entertaining, but 'watching' a book in this way offers little interaction, and has no real advantages over a printed edition plus an audio cassette of the narration. Perhaps such glossy CD-ROM books will continue to be published purely for the high-profile, shop-window effect, but it's not a type of publication that has a real future on CD.

Chapter 10
Leisure and Entertainment

- Magazines
- Comics
- Interactive movies
- Classical music
- Pop music
- Games

Introduction

There's a good deal of talk nowadays about the future of entertainment being an interactive one. Computer games will become more like interactive movies, it is said, and indeed movie-making techniques will adapt to allow for interactivity. So instead of simply watching Schwarzenegger in his latest blockbuster, you will be able to play Arnie's part, and make decisions about what he does that affect the plot and the outcome of the film.

The gurus who predict that we will no longer be happy to sit passively in front of our TVs, also say that we will want to take control over the music we're listening to. Instead of just taking what the artists throw at our ears, we'll want to get involved by changing and remixing the music, so that we share in the creative process.

If you're so inclined, you can see CD-ROM as the first step towards this interactive future of entertainment. You don't have to look at it that way, though, to realise that CD-ROM does bring several excellent new forms of entertainment.

Two in particular stand out. Enhanced CD-ROM games are getting more impressive all the time, and are genuinely at the forefront of interactive entertainment, while interactive CD-ROM albums are just beginning to explore some intriguing new ideas. We'll look at both of those in this chapter, as well as a few other interesting forms of CD-ROM entertainment.

Magazines

Just as non-fiction and reference book publishers have begun to explore the new medium of CD-ROM, seeing it as a viable future alternative to traditional print, magazine publishers also have begun to explore the possibilities of CD-ROM.

There's one very important reason why magazine publishers are keen to find out how well they can get their publications to work in an interactive medium, and that's networks. There's a widespread belief that on-line delivery of multimedia into the home via cable networks will take a significant portion of the market in current years, with the advantage for the publishers that there is no actual media cost – they won't have to print either paper or CD editions. From the user's point of view, there's the advantage that the information can be constantly updated, so that whenever you download a story you can be certain that it is 'hot off the presses', though it seems inevitable that the overall cost will be higher than the price of a newspaper, especially if you're tempted to check regular updates. On-line editions of newspapers like the Washington Post are already being tried on the Internet in America.

Magazines are a slightly different type of publishing, relying less on immediacy or 'up-to-dateness' and more on substance, so it's quite possible that even in a future in which all households were using on-line cable services, there will still be a place for magazines in a 'static' medium like CD-ROM. The user might be willing to pay a higher price for the initial purchase, knowing that he or she would be getting

Time Magazine's Desert Storm: War in the Persian Gulf is more than just a collection of articles. It works well, but Time is not yet ready to become a regular interactive publication.

good value because there would be more material on the CD than could easily be downloaded from an on-line news service.

Whatever the future for CD-ROM journalism, it's certainly true that electronic publishing of magazines is already with us. You're probably already aware that an increasing number of computer magazines are available with a cover-mounted CD-ROM, but it's only in rare cases (like *CD-ROM Today*) that these magazines are experimenting with the idea of publishing complete, stand-alone multimedia articles on their cover-mounted discs.

More intriguing is the example set by non-computer titles who have tried CD publishing, and two particular American magazines, *Newsweek* and *Time*, have led the way. *Time* was an obvious candidate for spearheading electronic publishing, since the Time Warner group has interests in many different kinds of media including films, TV and music publishing, and has long been active in exploring new media (initially through a division that was actually called Warner New Media). Similarly, *Newsweek* have in the past explored laserdisc publication, before settling on CD-ROM as a better bet.

Neither *Time* nor *Newsweek* has yet to attempt publishing a weekly or fortnightly magazine. Instead, *Newsweek Interactive* is published quarterly and contains the entire text of three months (13 issues) of the weekly magazine, plus audio recordings of all *Newsweek on Air* radio broadcasts, fronted by a set of specially-generated multimedia articles. *Time* has not set itself a strict schedule at all: instead it has published occasional one-off CD-ROM editions to cover specific topics, such as the War in the Gulf, under the tag-line 'first draft of history'.

The *Newsweek* and *Time* publications that have appeared to date have been very successful, not trying anything too elaborate with the interfaces but providing a solid resource of textual material that is enlivened by good quantities of audio and photographs. They've certainly proved it can be done, and done well.

Some people will tell you that someday soon we'll all carry miniaturised CD-ROM computers, akin to portable CD players or Sony's Data Discman idea. Even out and about, on a railway journey, we'll buy our magazines on CD-ROM from the station newsstand and we'll sit there on the train 'interacting' rather than just reading. This prediction might well prove to be true.

Certainly one big hurdle has been successfully negotiated by the electronic magazine, because Newsweek Interactive has already carried interactive advertisements which, apparently, a significant majority of users did actually choose to look at. Now there's a challenge for the advertising industry.

Comics

If magazines, why not comics on CD-ROM? Well, in part the same argument about fiction applies. A good computer game is very close to being an interactive comic, as *Beneath A Steel Sky*, with artwork by Dave Gibbons (of 2000AD and Watchmen fame) has demonstrated.

Comic Book Confidential – giving you pop art in a truly popular and up-to-date form. Fantastic.

All the same, if you are a comics enthusiast there are already several publications which will appeal to you, such as the history of comic art provided by *Comic Book Confidential*, or the interactive version of Art Spiegelman's graphic novel *Maus*.

Interactive movies

Apart from Video CD (see separate chapter) and the type of games that are classed as 'interactive movies', there have been some experiments in putting movies into a CD-ROM format. Examples include the 1994 release of a full-length animated cartoon feature in the Japanese 'Manga' style, and Voyager's CD-ROM interpretation of the Beatles movie *A Hard Day's Night*.

The success of movie discs like this is limited, simply because the movie window on a PC or Mac screen is far from being the ideal way of watching a movie. There are some interesting additions, though – the Beatles movie on CD-ROM, for example, includes extended biographical details and still photos of the Beatles as well as biogs of the other actors and further material by the same director. It also

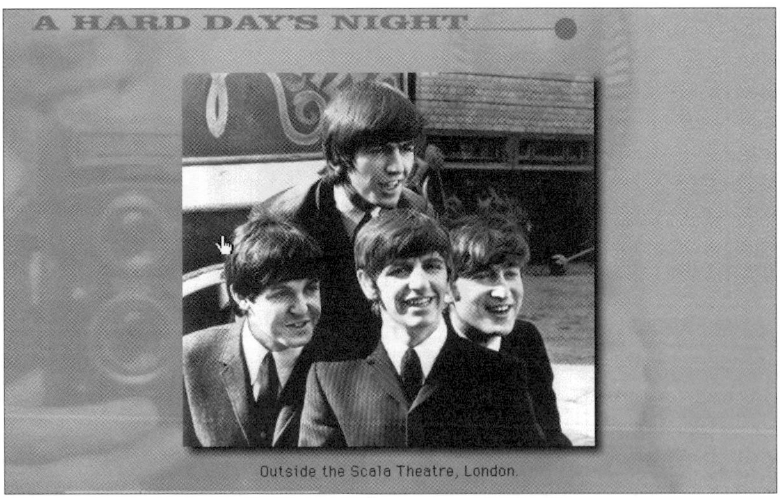

A Hard Day's Night – the interactive features are intriguing, but the video is not yet capable enough.

features the entire script of the film, with notes that show where pieces were changed or ad-libbed during shooting, and it gives you complete control over the movie so that you can read a line from the script, or listen to one of the songs, and jump to the point in the movie where that line or song occurs.

So you might find a movie disc interesting because of these additional features, even though it's not really practical to simply sit back and enjoy the film on a CD-ROM format. The other drawback is that there are very few movies released in this format to date.

Classical music

It's not just pop music that could be revolutionised by the addition of interaction. Classical music has long faced a major hurdle, which CD-ROM could help it to overcome. The classics have become increasingly popular over the last few years, but the beginner who starts off by simply enjoying the music soon finds himself or herself wanting to be better able to understand the music and to progress to more 'difficult' pieces, which tend to be the preserve of the musically

Beethoven's 5th, an interactive symphony from Mindscape, is perfectly happy to explain to you how an orchestra is structured, showing videos of individual instruments and sections.

educated minority. What are the ordinary man and woman in the street to do when tantalised by the promised rewards of difficult pieces like Stravinsky's *Rite of Spring*, and yet put off because they are all too aware that they lack the knowledge which would help them 'appreciate' the music?

It's this knowledge gap, between liking classical music and being able to really understand it, that CD-ROM can help to fill. The CD can not only supply a good recording of the music, but can also be used to supply a running commentary that explains what's going on as the music plays. And if you'd also like to see the score while the music plays, or read a biography of the composer, or receive an explanation of the instruments of the orchestra that are used in the piece, then all these things can be supplied with ease too.

This is really a terribly simple function for CD-ROM, but it's one of those (like encyclopedias and children's books) which immediately makes sense and, in some form or other, is certainly here to stay. You can already get a range of music in this form, from the obvious Beethoven's *5th* to Mozart, Schubert and Stravinsky, and I'd be willing to bet there will be many other titles to follow.

Interactive popular music

This is one of those areas that has helped CD-ROM gain a high profile. In 1994, Peter Gabriel's interactive album *Xplora 1*, for example, was the subject of a large article in the Sunday Times as well as appearing in music magazines like Q and, of course, in the computer press. When people like David Bowie, Prince and Todd Rundgren (all of whom released CD-ROMs in 1994) start exploring the artistic possibilities of a medium, you know it has a future.

One of the best things about interactive music, though, is that none of these artists was especially successful in their exploration of it, which leaves plenty of room for improvement and innovation. The temptation, inevitably, is for the musicians to see it as a mixed-media delivery system with which they can get the message over in the same old ways, and not to test its own special creative potential.

So the major fault of the first generation of interactive albums is that they were used to repackage existing material. Take Bowie's disc *Jump* as an example. It features several videos for songs from his *Black Tie, White Noise* album. It has a slideshow of photographs with a commentary by Bowie describing the making of the album, and it also has a set of video extracts from interviews with Bowie. And really, that is more or less your lot. All decent material, but all of it quite capable of being presented in a video, or some other traditional form.

There are, however, a few other ideas being played with in these early interactive albums which might be further developed in the future by musicians who want to become multimedia artists. One idea in particular stands out, and that's giving the user the ability to actually change the music. On Gabriel's disc, you can use an on-screen studio console to remix one of the tracks, altering the levels of eight different instrument and vocal tracks. On Bowie's disc you can do the same, and you can also create your own version of the *Jump* video, choosing sequences from five different source tapes and editing them into your own Bowie video. It's clever, but as yet it's not entirely a successful idea, though I did enjoy remixing the Bowie song.

The other idea that has great potential is what we'll have to call the 'virtual environment', for want of a better phrase. In the Gabriel disc, for instance, you can wander into the Real World studios (ironic, that name, in the circumstances) to meet musicians and see how everything works. Gabriel has also incorporated an adventure-game style mission into the disc, so that by collecting various items as you explore, you can gain access to 'hidden' parts of the disc.

Bowie's disc also has a virtual environment: you start by going up in a lift into an office building, and from the corridor you see three doors. You can visit the office, where the *Jump* video is played on a screen, and the slideshow of photos and the interview are to be found). You can whizz down the corridor into the recording studio, where you remix the song and the video. And there's also a third room, where you can look out of the window to see another song video being played on an advertising hoarding: from this room you can also 'jump' into two apartments in the building across the road, where there are various little 'click to activate' things happening (very reminiscent of the children's interactive storybooks) such as a piano or a guitar which you click on to hear a little snatch of melody. You can also find more song videos in these apartments, for instance by switching on the television.

This 'virtual environment' in Bowie's disc is not entirely successful – it's a little short on atmosphere, and really it's also far too small, because it inevitably invites comparison with the excellent adventure games we're all used to – but it offers some interesting ideas. In particular, the developers have tried very carefully to integrate themes from the videos, such as the antiseptic, harsh environment of the office, which picks up on themes in the *Jump* video. This is a step in the direction of the 'virtual environment' becoming an integrated part of the artist's creative concept, so that it ties the whole album together

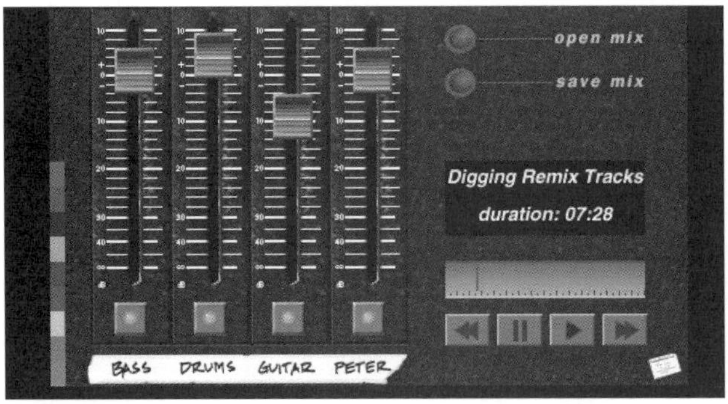

You can mix your own version of a Peter Gabriel track in Xplora1 (above), and David Bowie's Jump lets you do the same. Nevertheless, both discs are interactive rehashes of already released music.

The Residents' Freak Show – as soon as you find your way into the hidden depths, it's a multimedia extravaganza. A weird, interesting and highly original piece of interactivity.

and develops an atmosphere atmosphere and a 'feel' which enhances the traditional material. In other words, if it's done well, with the musician working closely with the multimedia developers, the interactive album could become an intriguing artistic creation that picks up on the spirit of the music and enhances it by building it into an atmospheric whole.

Interestingly enough, the best example of the interactive album that we've yet seen is one that pre-dates all the big names, and yet goes much, much further with this idea of creating a virtual world that suits and enhances the music. It's a disc called *Freak Show* created by Californian artist-musicians The Residents, and it's well worth a look for anyone who's interested in the future of interactive music because it is full of good ideas.

For starters, *The Residents' Freak Show* hides its substance away. Really it's an album of music videos, but you wouldn't know that when you first start exploring it. Instead, you enter a circus tent and watch a series of sideshows starring bizarre freaks of nature, the whole thing created as animations using 3D modelling techniques. It's all very weird and seems almost completely pointless, and I've known many people to give up at this point.

What you have to do, though, is find your way behind the scenes (literally), where you come across the sideshow freaks in their caravans. Here you can find out more about each freak, which is a bizarre experience, as well as discovering the strange, cartoon music videos (each song is about a particular freak).

There are also several other things to find, including an archive of Residents album releases and video clips from live performances, and there's even a book-like section in which you choose to read about different real-life historical circus freak acts.

For its atmosphere, its variety and its integration of the music videos into an environment that enhances them, *Freak Show* is a notable point in the history of interactive music. In 100 years' time, it'll be getting pride of place in museums of interactive art.

So, there's some intriguing stuff to be found in the area of interactive music, but there's probably better to come as other artists pick up on the successes of their predecessors and take them further. There's a lot to look forward to.

Introducing CD-ROM games...

We've already mentioned in a previous chapter that the first CD-ROM games for the PC and Mac were released in 1989, and this is indeed the case. Five years on much has changed, but other things have stayed the same.

One of those '89 vintage games was *The Manhole* for the Macintosh, which wasn't really a game at all, but nevertheless has had a distinct influence on the development of CD-ROM entertainment. It was a point-and-click explorative thing for kids which was the precursor of all the excellent children's books that you now find on CD-ROM. Its creators went on to produce a more advanced children's title along the same lines, called *Cosmic Osmo*, but they are best known nowadays for

LucasArts' Rebel Assault – released early in 1994, it helped the significant upswing in sales of CD-ROM drives, and was one of the better action/shoot-em-up type titles available.

the amazing and atmospheric game *Myst*, released for PC and Mac in 1984 and already a classic.

The other 1989 release was *Defender of the Crown* for the PC, which at the time seemed to be quite a dramatic development in gaming but which swiftly proved to be an evolutionary dead-end. Essentially it was exactly the same as the floppy disk version that already existed, except that it featured some extra animation, and used CD-DA sound to provide some rather nice music and sound effects.

Many of the CD-ROM games that are now available follow the same pattern. They are 'enhanced' versions of existing games, which is sometimes a good thing, but often makes no real gain over the floppy-disk versions of the game. Some 'enhanced' titles add only a fancy intro animation and some CD-DA music for the CD version, which really does not make good use of the CD-ROM at all.

Other enhanced titles make more sense, for both practical and artistic reasons. LucasArts' *Sam and Max Hit the Road*, for example, is simply more convenient on CD-ROM. Like many top-notch adventure games it fills 12 or 14 floppies and takes up about 30Mb of hard disk space in its non-CD form. But it also uses CD-DA audio to replace the the on-screen text with proper dialogue, acted out by real actors, which makes the experience of playing the game far more enjoyable.

Other games will use the space afforded by CD-ROM to add extra value. There are, for instance, compilations of up to 20 games on a single CD, which can be great value. An alternative to the mixed compilation is the game-plus-missions idea, where you buy not only the original game (flight sims and golf games are good examples) but also all the extra disks (missions, or golf courses) on one CD-ROM, and the whole package again has the benefit of good value.

The standard-bearers for CD-ROM, however, are neither the enhanced titles nor the compilations, but the CD-ROM-native productions. These are games specifically developed for CD-ROM, taking advantage of the immense storage space by integrating lots of animation and sound into the gameplaying experience.

Towards the end of 1993 and the beginning of 1994, CD-ROM games of this type started to change the entire course of games development. PC CD-ROM in particular was at the forefront, with titles like *The 7th Guest*, which actually filled two discs, and LucasArts' *Rebel Assault*, prompting many a user to invest in a CD-ROM drive, and persuading many console game-players to upgrade to a multimedia PC.

Interactive movies?

The phrase 'interactive movie' is heavily over-used, but many of the most innovative CD-ROM games titles certainly incorporate cinematic elements. In some cases, the producers of games have started 'filming' rather than 'programming' their games.

Rebel Assault, for example, draws on LucasArts' movie-making experience and resources and incorporates many video clips within the game. There are non-interactive video sequences featuring Star Wars characters like Luke, Darth Vader and the famous droids C3P0 and R2-D2, and these video clips act as links between the sections of the game, and which also develop the plot and build up the atmosphere. But even the game recreates the action from the Star Wars movies, with one of the key sections being the Death Star trench run.

Rebel Assault is an action game, and though the video helps the atmosphere along, it can't really be incorporated into the gameplay. All the same, the game sequences in *Rebel Assault* are very much like simulations, and so they too have a movie-like quality, so the whole thing integrates well. It's more of a surprise to see video clips being used in a cerebral, strategy-style game like *Sim City*, where the video clips might be atmospheric, but will inevitably stand out as being rather different from the non-realistic presentation of the actual game. Nonetheless, *Sim City Enhanced* is one of the most outstanding examples of a CD-ROM game, even if the movie element is only the icing on the cake.

When it comes to adventure games, however, the movie format can be wholeheartedly integrated into the gameplay. There are adventures now appearing which are actually filmed using real actors, making the

Return to Zork used real actors and actresses to create more lifelike graphics and to add speech, but remains a typical adventure.

whole development process far more like a movie production than a traditional game. A good example is *Return to Zork*, starring Jason Hervey (The Wonder Years) and Sam Jones (Flash Gordon) who both act out roles in this role-playing game.

There's also an increasing use of actors for narration, playing the characters in audio if not visually. Big names like Mark Hamill and Tim Curry crop up in Gabriel Knight, while the CD-ROM *Star Trek* game actually features most of the original cast. And with actors' narration providing the voices for the cartoon characters, LucasArts' *Sam and Max* is getting very close to being an interactive cartoon movie.

And finally, something completely different...

CD-ROM also has the potential to mix, match and invent rather new forms of entertainment: things that aren't really games, and are not exactly music, and really you couldn't call books.

How would you categorise, for instance, a disc like Professor Marvin Minsky's *Society of Mind*? It's one of the less successful titles in the highly adventurous Voyager range, but it's still intriguing: a kind of interactive documentary, I suppose, in which the professor explains his theories of how the mind works and how that relates to artificial intelligence. It's a peculiar disc, but it's not alone – there are many deeply quirky productions available on CD-ROM, which is one of the beauties of the medium. It's young enough for people still to be playing around with it and seeing what it can do.

Drama is also represented on CD-ROM. At the academic end of the spectrum there is, for instance, Arthur Miller's *The Crucible* explored through both performance and the text, with the actors of a respected theatre company explaining their approach. But what about *Karaoke Macbeth*? It's one of the silliest-sounding titles yet conceived, but perhaps CD-ROM could find a major educational niche by

Something completely different – Monty Python proves that comedy as well as music might find new creative forms thanks to interactive media.

presenting drama in which you can take the part of a leading character. Act-along-a- Gielgud might be just around the corner.

The royal family, Woodstock, John Lennon, World Cup soccer, Barbie dolls… all these are appearing on CD-ROM, and there's plenty more interesting stuff that we really don't have time to go into. But I'd just like to mention the first couple of discs released during

Not surprizingly, World Cup Soccer made its way onto CD-ROM in 1994.

1994 by a team calling themselves 7th Level. Their first release, *TuneLand*, was a disc of twenty popular children's songs arranged, performed and produced by top-name pop musicians including Pink Floyd's Scott Page and Dave Gilmour, Jon Andersen from Yes, and many others too numerous to mention. As well as being able to play the songs in an audio CD player, you can stick the disc in a CD-ROM drive and play an interactive children's book that incorporates all the songs. The follow-up to this is, believe it or not, a multimedia Monty Python adventure. Now that's what I call completely different!

Karaoke

It's not everyone's idea of a good evening in (or out, for that matter) but I feel it only fair to mention that not only is CD-ROM's mixture of CD-DA music and graphics ideal for karaoke, but also the Video CD standard bears a close relationship to the Philips/JVC Karaoke CD standard. As a result there are a number of karaoke discs available on all popular CD-ROM formats. You have been warned or advised, whichever way you look at it. I'll say no more, other than to point out that if you want to keep the kids out of harm's way but don't mind them making a bit of noise, there are quite a few kids' karaoke discs available, and the sprogs might enjoy themselves singing along with Old MacDonald's Farm and the like. At least they should be able to stay clean that way, so maybe it's better than letting them out in the garden.

PD and shareware collections

We've put this under the heading of 'entertainment' purely because it had to go somewhere! Besides which, many of the collections of PD and shareware programs that are available on CD-ROM do happen to feature large numbers of games. Some, indeed, are purely games.

A CD-ROM can hold hundreds of shareware and freeware programs, so inevitably there are quite a few collections on the market that feature hundreds of individual programs. These are lucky dips in several senses – the £20 or so that such discs cost could prove to be good value if you find just a couple of games you enjoy or utilities that you find useful, but you'll have to dig through a lot of dross to find these.

You'll also find that the computer magazines are very unlikely to carry reviews of PD and shareware collections, simply because the contents are so diverse that it would take an age to look through the whole lot. It's also fair to say that when they come across interesting examples of shareware, the magazines are very likely to put them on their cover-mounted CDs anyway, since such programs take up only a small proportion of the disc.

To reduce the hit-or-miss aspect a little, you will find that there are collections of PD software of specific types – games for Windows, for instance, or Internet-related programs. If you're into a really serious subject like C programming, you might well find that shareware collections can supply you with things you simply couldn't get anywhere else.

Chapter 11

Down to business

- Clip media
- DIY multimedia
- CD-Recordable

Examples of Photo CD images that can be imported into your own paint packages or DTP documents.

Introduction

Many business applications use CD-ROM as a storage medium for large quantities of rapidly-searchable text. Obvious examples include the entire UK phone book, published by BT at around £1,000, as well as mailing lists and catalogues. Some large retail organisations publish their own parts lists and mail order catalogues on CD-ROM, though clearly you have to have quite a few outlets before it's economically viable to produce such a catalogue – and yet if your firm is already putting the man-hours into compiling extensive lists, it might be cheaper and more efficient to distribute them on CD-ROM than it is to produce them on paper.

In this book, we're not really in a position to say much more than that about this particular use of CD-ROM. Instead, this chapter will concentrate on two other aspects: firstly, enhanced CD-ROM versions of familiar productivity applications; second, and most importantly, the ways in which you can create your own multimedia presentations, perhaps for use in point-of-information or point-of-sale systems.

Enhanced CD-ROM applications

Because application programs need to work in RAM, there will always be a limitation on the amount of space a program takes up, and in any case smaller programs run faster, so CD-ROM cannot be used to store larger, better versions of the actual software. It makes no sense. But since CD is a cheaper delivery medium than floppy disks anyway, there are other things you can do to use up all the space on a CD-ROM. In an enhanced CD-ROM application, the extra storage space is used for two things.

First of all, it can be used to provide multimedia tutorials which show novices how to use the package, and so help to reduce the need for expensive training. So far one of the only programs to use this approach is Microsoft's *Works for Windows* in its CD-ROM version, although *PC Plus* magazine in its CD-ROM edition has made some interesting experiments with offering tutorials for specific, popular applications.

Tutorials might be a bright idea, but the other approach is far more common, and that is to use the space on the CD-ROM to store lots of extra clip media. Now it's not a lot of use getting other people's spreadsheets or databases with your application, so it's publishing and illustration software that has so far benefited from this approach.

Probably the best example is Corel Draw for the PC, which in its CD-ROM edition comes with an enormous library of images that you can load into the package to edit or simply use in DTP or WP (Word Processor) documents. The package also comes with a manual which has all the images printed out, so it's pretty easy to find out if the image you want is to be found on the disc, and where to find it.

Clip art, fonts and media libraries

Another logical use for the storage capacity of CD-ROM is to provide vast libraries for all kinds of program data. The most obvious example is clip-art libraries which provide images for use in DTP, word processing and graphics work. Such collections are able to supply large quantities of data at a comparatively low price – the CD will store the equivalent of over 450 high-density floppy disks and yet materially cost about the same to make as two disks would.

You can buy collections of structured (object-oriented) images in the format of particular illustration programs, or even Postscript images, or you can buy bitmap images in popular formats like TIF, GIF, PCX and PICT. As well as computer-generated artwork, things like backgrounds (marble, wood and stone textures, for instance) are available in CD-ROM collections, as are photographs, either using standard bitmap file formats or using Kodak's Photo CD format.

Some of the clip-art discs in particular, are collections of shareware or freely distributable images from the public domain, but most discs that contain collections of images are produced for commercial gain, and while the images are intended for royalty-free use, you do have to take a pretty careful look at the copyright conditions that are attached. In almost all cases, the copyright remains with the artist or photographer, and you will be restricted from using the images in documents with a print run of over 20,000 copies, or on covers.

Another thing that's important in DTP, word processing and graphic design, and is also important in video and in multimedia production, is which typefaces you use, and libraries of fonts are also available on CD-ROM. There are some discs that are collections of shareware or freeware typefaces, which are good value at about £20 or £30. There are also more expensive complete collections of fonts where you buy a disc and can use all the fonts on the disc, but these are likely to be inferior cuts of the typefaces.

If you want professional-quality fonts, CD-ROM is now the most popular way to gain access to the fonts in a top-name library, but you will usually not buy the whole library. You will usually have to pay separately for each single typeface on a disc, generally by telephoning for an unlock code, so that you can copy the font to your hard drive,

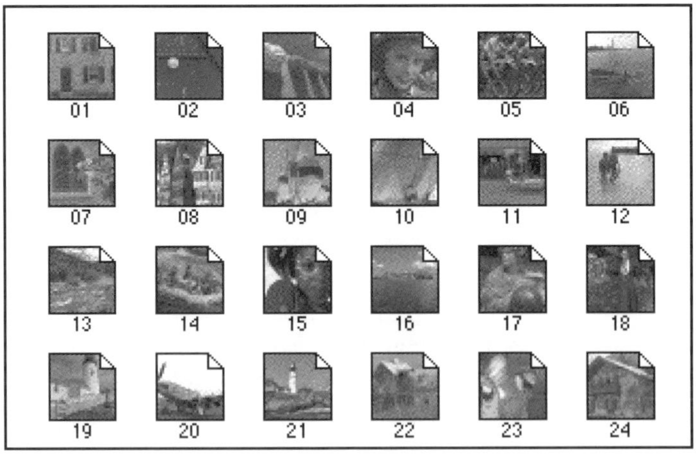

On a Mac, you can easily look through a library of Photo CD images at thumbnail size. Many clip media discs also offer brousing interfaces to help you find pictures according to their content.

and paying by credit card. If you're feeling extravagant, however, you could splash out on an entire disc containing all the typefaces of a big-name font library, which will cost several thousand pounds and upwards.

With many people now wishing to produce their own multimedia, there is also a wide choice of discs containing video, sound and music clips. Again these are usually royalty-free within certain restrictions. The subjects vary widely: you can happily buy video clips of NASA's space missions, for instance, though why you would want to incorporate spacewalks and rocket launches into your own presentations is a bit of a mystery. Video clips are usually in .AVI format for PC and QuickTime for Mac, with PC sound and music clips usually provided as .WAV files.

Why DIY multimedia?

There's a wide range of programs on offer which will help you to create your own multimedia applications or presentations. It's hard to say exactly who might want to do this, but presumably, since the programs are on sale, there are a reasonable number of people who do want to. For business purposes, for instance, you might well use a multimedia presentation to replace a traditional sales pitch or audio-visual presentation. In any business that has dealings with the public, or in institutions like libraries and museums, point-of-sale and point-of-information presentations can be used to help customers find out about products or services.

If your business is sufficiently large, point-of-sale could be well worth exploring. It's long been rumoured that Argos catalogue showrooms, for example, have been planning to go over to a point-of-sale multimedia system to replace the use of catalogues in-store, with the advantage that the PoS system could also take orders. Similar 'interactive buying' systems are already in use at airport duty-free locations. As this book goes to press, Rover are putting the finishing touches to their own PoS system, with which the customer can choose detailed specifications of model, colour, trim level and so forth, and then see his or her chosen car 'in action' in a video. And there are quite a few museums using interactive presentations.

What you need to make your own multimedia

The actual production process involved in creating a multimedia application or presentation is not a million miles away from DTP. You'll need a specific multimedia authoring application – a range of choices is outlined below – with which to actually put the presentation together, which is analogous to the DTP package. The rest of the work is all preparation of materials, so you'll need graphics software to process images and something to create words with. You may also find it useful to have software that you can use to edit sounds, and if you want too use video, you'll probably need to add a video capture card.

Of course you'll need a PC or Mac to work on, and you'll also need much more RAM than is normal – about 16Mb is ideal – because you'll be doing some intensive graphics work. You'll also need a very large hard drive on which to store all the data you're using, so if you plan to fill a whole 650Mb CD, you'll probably need to get a 1 Gigabyte hard disk drive.

If you want to distribute your multimedia presentation, you'll have to consider how you will be publishing the CD-ROM. You can send it off to a duplication firm to be mastered and produced, which is quite economical even for small runs, in which case you'll have to ensure that your 1Gig hard drive is not only removable, but also safely portable. An alternative would be to get a CD-R machine with which to write your own CDs, and with prices as low as £2,000 for a machine and £20 for the recordable discs this may be a good option – though remember that you will also need another large hard drive to create an 'image' of the CD on at the mastering stage.

Finally, you'll have to think about where the disc is going to be played. If you want to set up point-of-sale or point-of-information stations, then the cost will be high. Each station will need a multimedia PC or Mac of sufficient specification to run your disc, and you'll probably want to replace the ordinary monitor with a touch-screen so that users don't have to use the mouse.

The basics of multimedia authoring

The basic principles of an interactive presentation are really very simple. A screen of information is presented on the display of the computer, and the information it contains could be text, graphics or video. From this first screen, the user should be able to choose to see other screens of information by clicking on areas of the screen. And that's really all there is to it – the rest of the application is simply a repetition of the same, basic mechanism.

So a multimedia authoring program can be pretty simple in operation, too. You will open a presentation window in which to work on the first screen of your presentation, and you can then import graphics, video clips or text and place them on the screen. Most authoring software will also enable you to type in text directly, and to create simple graphics like coloured shapes or boxes. You can generally also resize, and possibly even edit, imported graphics.

Once the screen is arranged to your satisfaction, you then have to define which areas of it are 'active' – in other words, which areas of the screen will make something happen when you click on them. Usually you can choose to draw out invisible active areas over the screen, though you can normally also choose to place buttons or menus on the screen instead. Finally, you have to set what will happen when each active area is clicked on by the user, which at its most basic means choosing which screen will appear if the active area is clicked on. Then all you have to do is repeat this process for other screens.

So in principle multimedia authoring is quite simple, but in practice, of course, it can get rather more difficult – not because there's anything complicated involved, but more because of the quantity of information, and the number of connections, that you have to be able to deal with.

Different approaches to authoring

The key aspect of how a multimedia authoring program works is the way it enables you to handle the interaction. In other words, how you set what happens when the user clicks on an active area on the screen.

When you're looking at Windows CD-ROM software, you'll generally find that the application has been programmed from scratch, like a game, or put together using a custom tool created by the developers. On the Mac, though, it's rather different. Many Mac CD-ROM titles have been created using an authoring package that you can buy and use yourself – and the vast majority of them have been created using a package called *Director*.

The strange thing about this is that *Director* was never actually intended to be used as an authoring system. It's actually an animation sequencing package that just happened to allow for the user to affect the flow of the animation.

In essence, *Director* enables you to lay out a huge long sequence of video 'events' – screens of text and pictures, animations or videos, which can be static or moving. Using a scripting language called Lingo, you can then organise jumps from one point in the sequence to another, which is how your interaction is added.

Scripting languages are a common feature of multimedia authoring packages. Essentially, a scripting language is just like a collection of DOS commands, so if you understand how to use DOS, you should be able to use a scripting language. Mac owners who've never found

Director is used by 50,000 multimedia developers worldwide but its interface is tricky to learn. The functions of your multimedia presentation – basically, what it shows on the screen or plays through the speakers – are represented in a huge, long list called a sequence, and choices that the user can make are controlled by a scripting language that tells the application when to jump to a different point in the sequence. Originally a Mac application, Macromedia have recently released a Windows version of Director.

their way round a command line interface (one that requires you to type in commands in order to use the computer) might find it a little more tricky, but the principles of a scripting language are simple enough and if you have a logical mind, you should pick it up quickly. Not all multimedia authoring packages use a scripting language, but all the most powerful ones tend to, because scripts are very powerful ways of accessing the inner workings of the computer's operating system.

Since *Director* is already used by about 50,000 multimedia developers worldwide its effectiveness is proven, and the latest version, *Director 4*, can be used on either Mac or PC to develop applications that will run on both platforms. It is, however, a very difficult package to learn to use, because it has a very complex interface – and it costs around £1,200.

The same 'video sequencer' approach used by *Director* (Computers Unlimited, 081 200 8282) is also used by some other, cheaper, multimedia authoring packages. The *Multimedia Workshop* (Ablac, 0626 332233) costs only £60 and is available for the Mac only. It uses a similar, but vastly less complex, video sequencer approach, the only drawback being that it doesn't really allow the use to make choices and jump to different sections, so while it will create linear multimedia presentations, it's not really any good for interactive multimedia.

Another similar package is *Q/Media 2* (AKQA, 0344 872472) for the PC only, which costs £130 and, like *Director*, has been developed from a strictly linear presentation program. With this one you first create your individual screen, then add buttons to it for the user's interaction, setting what happens when the button is activated. The overall shape of your whole presentation is shown in an outline window which shows the order in which the screens will be displayed, and also shows the links between various screens. This is quite a simple and effective system, and though *Q/Media* is possibly not quite powerful enough for professional authoring, it's a good package.

The real drawback of all of these video sequencer systems, however, including the all-powerful *Director*, is that they are not ideally suited to handling the logic of interactive multimedia, where the ability to 'branch' (in other words, make several choices) can lead to complicated logical structures. The makers of *Director*, Macromedia, put some thought into solving this problem and came up with an alternative approach in the form of *Authorware*.

Authorware (Peritas, 0753 868181) is the program used by CD-ROM Today magazine to create presentations for its cover-mounted disc. It has the advantages that it's very simple to get to grips with, and you can create presentations on the Mac and port them over to the Windows PC (though they will need a little tidying up). Its main drawback is that the full version is inordinately expensive (about £4,000) because it's aimed at professional developers.

The *Authorware* approach involves using a flow chart to define the various branches and loops of the interaction. You place icons on the flow chart to represent different kinds of screen, then double-click the icon to make the screen it represents appear in the presentation

Of the three popular approaches to multimedia authoring – Video Sequencer, HyperCard or flow chart – the latter is probably the most effective, and the easiest to understand. Authorware uses a flow chart approach, which makes the structure of the interaction obvious at all times. The key to it is the use of the decision icons which represent a choice offered to the user. In the presentation window you can create the screen which shows the choices to the user, and you can then add in the responses (moving to other screens, play a video, whatever) which takeplace when the user clicks on one of the icons you offer.

window. You can now import and place graphics, text and videos on the screen, then set active areas or buttons of various kinds.

The advantage of the flow chart system is that the consequences of each interaction are represented by icons on the flow chart, so that the whole logical structure of your presentation is always easily accessible. *Authorware* also includes a scripting language which you don't absolutely have to use, but which can help you do all sorts of things which might otherwise be rather tricky.

One package that uses a similar flow-chart approach is *MasterClass 2* (ISC, 0372 475226) which is somewhat cheaper than *Authorware* at a mere £1,169 but is for PC only. The difference with this one is that the flow-chart structure tends to be more complex and that it also incorporates some elements of a scripting language into the flow chart – you can type in commands on the flow-chart screen – which does make the flow look almost like a traditional program. Nonetheless, *MasterClass* is very simple to pick up and can be very effective, though in some respects it is not as powerful as Authorware.

As well as the two approaches to authoring we've seen already – the video sequencer and flow chart approaches – there is a third system

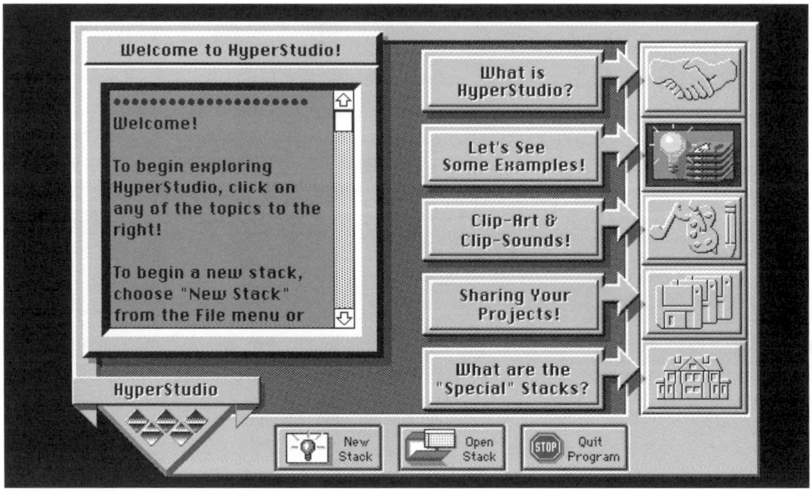

HyperStudio is a very simple version of the HyperCard approach – it tells you what to do as you go along.

which is popular for Mac authoring packages, and that's the *HyperCard* approach, named after Apple's original interactive application creator of several years ago. *HyperCard* was used to create things like the infamous *The Manhole*, but worked in black-and-white only. But the old *HyperCard*'s desecdants are full-colour and vastly more powerful, and this type of software was used by Peter Gabriel to create his *Xplora 1* disc.

The *HyperCard* system is terribly simple because it views the screens as 'cards' and the application as a 'stack' of these cards, the analogy being with something like the 'flash cards' used in primary schools, or slides in a slideshow. You can draw or write on each card (import text, graphics or videos, that is) then add buttons which will take the user to another card in the same stack, or to another stack.

HyperCard-style systems are terribly easy to use, and there are alternatives to the official Apple offering, though only for the Mac – no PC developers seem to have picked up on the idea. One such is *HyperStudio* (Tag, 0474 357350), which is cheap at only £160 or so and incredibly simple to use, though inevitably it is less powerful than a professional-standard system. There's a discount on this one for educational buyers, and it could well find a comfortable niche in schools thanks to its ease of use.

So your basic choice is between the three different approaches to multimedia authoring – the complex video sequencer idea, the simple but less powerful *HyperCard*-style system, or the flexible flow-chart approach. Once you've made that choice, you can then look through the options and find a package that fits your budget. Inevitably, the most expensive are best suited to professional use.

Other software that you'll need

As well as the authoring software, you'll also need several programs to prepare all the text, pictures and so on. What you need for video is discussed below, so we'll ignore that for the moment. Text shouldn't be a problem, because everyone has access to a word processor, and since all WP programs can save plain ASCII text there should be no problems with compatibility.

If you want to use sound effects and music you will often be able to use clips from a royalty-free disc supplied in the necessary PC or Mac file format, but if you want to create your own, or edit the ones you've acquired elsewhere, you'll need a decent sample-editing program. Most PC sound cards come with such software included. The best source of a Mac equivalent is usually a shareware program. To create your own music, you could also consider a sequencer program – again, simple ones are widely available as shareware.

Which leaves graphics as the main consideration. One important source of graphics for multimedia is Photo CD, which will help you get your own photos transformed into computer graphics files. The only alternative is a fairly expensive scanner. There are also an enormous range of royalty-free images available in Photo CD format.

Graphic Converter for the Mac (right) and Paint Shop Pro on the PC are both versatile and easy-to-use graphics programs, and both are shareware.

So you'll need the Photo CD access software, but you'll probably have that already. You then need a graphics program with which you can edit your pictures, so you'll need painting and drawing tools as well as features like cut-and-paste. And you'll also want to crop pictures to size, translate them to different file formats, reduce the number of colours in your images, convert them to black and white, and alter the contrast and brightness.

Many of these functions are offered by a good image processing program, and by a very lucky coincidence there happen to be excellent shareware image processors available for both Mac (*Graphic Converter*) and PC (*Paint Shop Pro*). Both these packages were included on *CD-ROM Today* Disc 2, if you have trouble tracking them down elsewhere.

Producing your own video clips

It's actually very easy to produce your own video clips for use in your own presentations. The process is one of 'digitising in' the video footage and storing it in computerised form on your hard disk drive. It's a process that is more or less identical to sound sampling, the main difference being that whereas the Mac already includes everything you need to sample sounds, and a PC sound card also adds the necessary sound-sampling hardware and software, neither machine normally has the ability to sample video.

There is one exception to this rule, and that's the AV range of Macs, which come with both the hardware and the software that you need. Since an AV model only costs about £200 more than the equivalent non-AV Mac, if you are likely to want to digitise video clips, then an AV model would be a good bet.

Otherwise, you'll have to add a hardware card to your Mac or PC, and the necessary software will be supplied along with the card. Video capture cards, as they're known, are pretty cheap on the PC – the Pro Movie Studio card from Media Vision, for instance, costs only £179 and comes with Video for Windows and the semi-professional authoring package *Authorware Star* (a version of *Authorware Professional* that is limited to 1,000 icons in the flow-chart). Cards for the Mac tend to be more expensive: the one Apple always mention in their advertisements, the VideoSpigot, costs a whacking £1,200 or so, but I'm assured that you can get Mac capture cards for as little as £200-300.

With the card and software installed, all you have to do is plug a video recorder in to the back of your computer using an appropriate cable, then play the video and record the bits you want using the video capture software. You video will be automatically stored to the hard drive using the AVI format on the PC or as a QuickTime movie on the Mac, complete with audio. The software usually enables you to edit the video afterwards, chopping out sequences you don't want, altering the number of colours if the video is taking up too much space and even dubbing in different audio.

Apart from the fact that videos can easily take up huge quantities of hard disk space, so that you have to play around with the frame rate and the number of colours to cut the files down to a manageable size, recording your video clips is actually a very simple and straightforward process.

CD-Recordable

Once you've created your multimedia presentation, you can either send it off to a duplicator to get a master disc made, or you can do it yourself using a writeable CD system. These systems were once known as WORM drives (Write Once, Read Many times) but are now generally known as CD-R (short for Recordable).

CD-R writers use gold-coloured, recordable discs which cost about £20 each. These discs are coated with a special greenish-coloured photo-sensitive lacquer on the underside, into which the data is etched by a powerful laser. Once used, the gold discs cannot be blanked and re-used. Gold discs are available in two sizes, representing either 63 minutes or 74 minutes of CD audio, which corresponds to either 580Mb or 640Mb of data storage.

CD-R machines are now widely available from lots of different big-name manufacturers. The only problem is that you can't simply plug the CD-R machine into your computer and write the data for your CD-ROM straight on to the disc.

First of all, you have to create an 'image' of the CD-ROM disc, which is a version of the data stored on a hard drive in the same format in which it will finally appear on the CD-ROM. This image behaves the same as a CD-ROM and can be tested for errors before the data is finally written to the CD-R disc.

CD-ROM Today use a JVC ROM-Maker system, which is expensive at about £7,000 but incorporates all the necessary software to build the image, as well as having an in-built hard drive on which the image can be built. This makes it an all-in-one system that saves considerable time and trouble.

CD-Recordable machines can cost as little as £2000, like the single speed Pinnacle 202 (top right). But you should consider paying more for a double speed CD writer like the Reflection Systems RF-4100 (bottom right) which, with a 2Mb data buffer, will not spoil discs if your hard drive thermally recalibrates (pauses to cool down) while 'burning' a disc.

Otherwise, you will have to buy another large hard drive on which to build the image, and here another problem crops up. When it comes to actually writing the disc, the CD-R machine requires a constant, uninterrupted flow of data, but most hard drives will pause occasionally – only for a few milliseconds, but it's enough – to cool down (a process known as 'thermal recalibration'). Hard disk drives that do not need to recalibrate are quite rare, but many CD-R systems will require you to track down such a hard drive. The documentation for the CD-R machine will usually suggest appropriate makes.

An alternative is to buy a CD-R machine with a data buffer, such as the Reflection Systems RF-4100, which costs £2,995. Other important things to look for in a CD-R machine are multi-tasking software that has the ability to cut a disc in the background, so that you can still use your computer while a disc is being written, and the ability to write discs at double speed, cutting down the time a disc takes to make from about three hours to only an hour and a half.

Chapter 12
Video CD

- How Video CD works
- Getting equipped

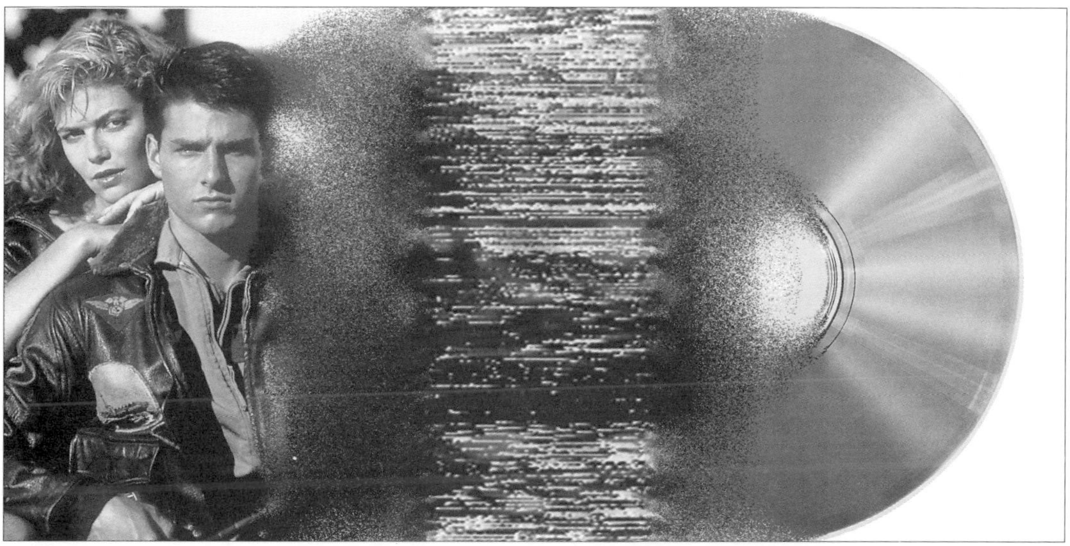

Introducing Video CD

Video CD is an increasingly widespread technology standard for playing video from ordinary 120mm compact discs which look just like audio CDs or CD-ROM discs, though of course the video discs use a different data format. In just the same way that a CD-ROM drive uses the same technology as an audio CD player, so too does the Video CD system – so a CD-ROM system can be adapted to play Video CD discs, and audio CD players can also be adapted.

Which means that Video CD players are currently available in a number of different forms. You can fit a hardware card that costs about £300 to a CD-ROM Mac or PC to enable the system to play Video CD discs. There are digital video cartridges that adapt the Philips CD-i and the Commodore Amiga CD32 so that they too can play Video CD discs. There are supposed to be adapter boxes coming onto the market which will adapt a hi-fi audio CD player to play Video CDs, though none has yet appeared. And you can now buy special, dedicated Video CD players, though the only commercially available one of these that I've seen to date is a Panasonic model which costs about £1,000 and incorporates the Video CD technology

Philips' CD-i with the addition of a £150 Digital Video Cartridge was the first machine on sale that could play Video CD discs.

into a hi-fi midi system, with an amplifier and speakers, so that the system can play audio cassettes, audio CDs and Video CDs (both the latter being placed in the same CD drive).

Philips were the first firm in the world to bring a Video CD player to market, with the Philips CD-i/Digital Video Cartridge combination, in late 1993. This system now costs £450 while the stand-alone CD-i is £299. Philips hoped that Video CD would give the CD-i a major commercial advantage, but of course they needed to have a range of discs available to play on the system, so Philips tied up a deal with Paramount to release about 20 movies, theoretically in time for Christmas '93. In fact, the titles have been appearing slowly ever since.

Currently, the most significant videos available in Video CD format are Philips' range of movies and a variety of music discs. Films now available include *Top Gun*, *Wayne's World*, *Hunt for Red October*, *Star Trek*, *Coming to America*, *A Fish called Wanda* and *Indecent Proposal.* Music video collections just released by Picture Music International include Pink Floyd, David Bowie, Tina Turner and Kate Bush while Philips offer Eric Clapton and Bryan Adams.

Video CD is picking up momentum at the moment, with a number of cult releases on the way including Bruce Lee movies and the Halloween series. Many experts in the video industry believe that Video CD will replace VHS video cassettes within three years, and it is widely said that the reason many top-name films will not be available for some while is that the film companies are holding back their top titles so that they can make more of a splash and cash in properly when a wider user base emerges.

There's one other aspect of Video CD that's worth a mention before we go on to look at how Video CD works, and that's the pleasantly nostalgic fact that only 65 minutes of digital video will fit on one disc, which means full-length feature films come on two discs, giving you

Some of the better Video CD performances available clockwise from top left: Wayne's World, The Naked Gun 2 1/2, Harrison Ford in Patriot Games, Jon Bon Jovi, Star Trek VI, and Top Gun.

the chance to make a cup of tea or have an ice-cream during the interval.

How Video CD works

The advantages of digital video are almost exactly like the advantages of digital audio on compact disc. It's much more controllable, so you can jump to any point on the disc, and it's more robust – unlike magnetic tape, it doesn't wear out over time. But while digital music has been around for a while, digital video posed rather more difficult technical problems which have only recently been solved.

As you know, moving pictures at the cinema and on TV give the illusion of movement by flicking rapidly through a series of slightly different pictures, or 'frames'. A digital video system needs to play at a rate of 25 frames every second, which is the frame rate that European PAL TV works at (American NTSC TV runs at 30 fps).

The problem is this. When you convert each picture to digital data – or computer data, it's exactly the same – you need a vast amount of data for each frame. Digital pictures work by storing a different number to represent the colour of each individual pixel on the screen. So even if you only had one bit of data – one binary one or zero – for each pixel on a 640-by-480 computer screen, you'd have 640 times 480 different pixels, which works out as 307,200 bits of data, the equivalent of 38,400 bytes or 37.5Kb. Just for one frame.

Unfortunately, CD drives can only transfer data at a limited speed. A single-speed drive works at around 150Kb per second, while a double-speed drive manages 300Kb per second. If each of the 25 frames of video you want to shift every second takes up 37.5Kb, then that means you need to transfer 937.7Kb every second, and of course you simply can't do it.

The trouble is made even worse by the fact that you actually need much more than just one bit of data for each coloured pixel on the TV screen, because only one bit per pixel means only black-and-white. If you have just one bit, that bit can be a one or a zero, and you can use that to represent two colours for the pixel – most obviously black or white. With two bits you have four different combinations, so you can have four different colours. With three bits, eight colours. With four, 16 colours. Five bits give 32 colours and so on, up to eight-bit (256 colours), 16-bit (65,536 colours) and full 24-bit (16,777,216 colours), which is called 'true colour' because it's

Kate Bush and Pink Floyd, two of the top names in music who have released video collections on CD.

considered to be as many different shades of colour as you could possibly need to represent any natural object.

Ideally, some time in the future, full 24-bit video would be the aim. In the meantime, it's generally accepted that 16-bit colour is good enough to give a picture quality that's substantially better than VHS tape, so that's the target. In actual fact, Video CD uses a 15-bit colour system to give 32,768 colours on-screen. Even then, one single frame of video needs to be about 300Kb of data, and to get 25 of those every second you'd need to be transferring more than 7Mb of data per second through a CD drive that can only manage 150Kb per second.

Simply devising a CD drive with faster transfer rates isn't really an option. Double-speed drives are now standard for CD-ROM, but going any faster than that is tricky (you start running into problems with the laser. The 'quad-speed' drives now just beginning to go on sale use a different colour of laser which makes them massively more expensive.

What you have to do instead, then, is reduce the amount of data you need to transfer. Obvious ways of doing this include cutting down the number of colours used to 256-colour 8-bit, or reducing the screen resolution so that there are fewer pixels, or running at a slower frame rate. Most made-for-TV cartoons, for example, use animation at only 12 frames per second. Computer game animation uses all three of these techniques.

Alternatively, you could reduce the size of the screen substantially so that the video only runs in a small window, which is how Video For Windows and the Apple's QuickTime system work.

The aim of Video CD, however, is to create what's called FMV – which, though it translates as 'Full-Motion Video', actually ought to be called 'full-screen, full-motion video'. You want full TV-like screen resolution, you want full TV-screen size, and you want to run at TV's 25 frames per second.

The answer is what's called compression, the same technique that enables you to squeeze twice as much data on floppy or hard disks. If you liken your data to orange juice, compression is the equivalent of boiling off all the water to give you concentrated orange juice, which you can then transport more easily. At the other end, you simply add water and end up with more or less what you started with.

Compression can be done using a number of different techniques. One, for example, works on the assumption that in the average picture you'll have broad areas that are the same colour, like the blue sky in a landscape – instead of repeating the information that says 'blue' for the first three hundred pixels, you just say 'pixel one is blue, and the next two hundred and ninety-nine are the same'.

Another important technique is called 'delta compression'. This works on the assumption that in a sequence of moving pictures, the changes from one frame to the next are often very slight. Instead of storing a whole new frame each time, you store the whole of the original one and thereafter say 'just change this area'.

The final problem is that you have plenty of time to compress the video data before you put it on to a compact disc, because you do it at the manufacturing stage, but you need to decompress it again very rapidly – 'on the fly' or 'in real time', as they call it – when the disc is playing. And that brings about a need for more clever electronic circuitry.

With all these problems to solve, a number of the world's major electronics companies decided to set up and co-fund a scientific research organisation, and share the results when the problem was cracked. The organisation is called MPEG, the Motion Picture Expert Group, and just before Christmas 1992 they announced that they had come up with something that worked.

The MPEG1 standard which they created is a system of compression techniques along with a specified design of microchip to do all the

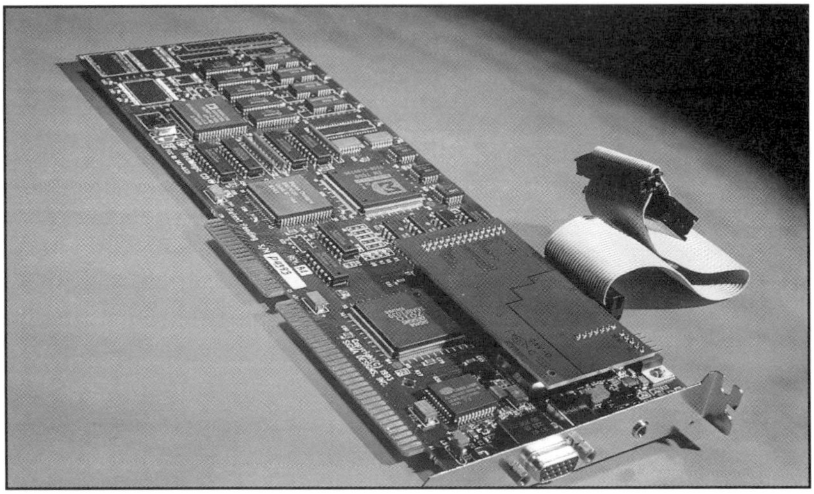

The RealMagic card by Sigma Designs will adapt your PC so that it can play MPEG files and Video CD discs. It's the first of what's expected to be a whole slew of MPEG cards to hit the market.

decompressing. However, even after the MPEG 1 standard was made available, it still needed a lot more work to turn MPEG1 into a finished consumer product, and this work went on throughout 1993.

Beyond digital video

One of the most interesting aspects of Video CD is that it is not only used for plain, straightforward videos. It can also be used to add proper full-screen, full-motion video to fully interactive CD-ROM applications that previously had to be satisfied with Video for Windows or QuickTime video clips.

Some popular CD-ROM games have already been released in Video CD full-motion versions, including *Return to Zork*, *Lord of the Rings*, *Space Ace*, *Dragon's Lair*, *The Horde* and *Conspiracy*. Specific interactive movie-style games using Video CD have been created, such as Philips's much-vaunted *Voyeur* for the CD-i. And FMV versions of big-name CD-ROM reference titles like *Compton's Interactive Encyclopedia* and Software Toolworks' *World Atlas* and *20th Century Video Almanac* are already available.

Getting Video CD equipped

The first Video CD card, or 'MPEG playback card', as it's known, was the RealMagic board for the PC from Sigma Designs, distributed in the UK at £249 plus VAT by Gem (0279 412441) and available through stores like Game, Escom and PC World. ReelMagic had the market to itself until well on into 1994, but a whole host of other cards are now becoming available, including ones for the Mac, so there's plenty of choice.

Apple have opened up another interesting new option with their TV Mac, the Performa or LC 630. As well as including a TV tuner and having a 15-inch monitor with stereo speakers, the 630 is designed for an official Apple Video CD plug-in.

Chapter 13
Kodak Photo CD

- How to use Photo CD
- Photo CD software

With Photo CD you can take your negatives or slides to boots, have your photos stored on a disc that you can put in your CD-ROM drive, then view and use your pictures on your computer.

Introducing Photo CD

Leaving aside, for the moment, the CD-ROM element, let's look at the stand-alone idea of Kodak Photo CD as Kodak is hoping to sell it in the high street – a new piece of consumer wizardry which is, in the words of a leaflet available from any branch of Boots, "an entirely new system which uses compact discs to store your colour photographs, and lets you view them on your television!". "Imagine seeing your own photos on TV," enthuses a leaflet available from Kodak processing shops, in a similar vein. "Well now you can."

First of all, you need a device to play Photo CDs on – a black box, looking like a video or like a hi-fi CD player, which you hook up to your telly. When the Photo CD system was first launched on the market, this would have set you back £299 at least. Once you have the black box player, you can get some photos put on to disc. This involves first buying the gold-coloured, recordable CD at £4.99 (it holds up to 100 images) and then paying around 60p each for the photos to be transferred from negatives or slides, so a set of 36 exposures plus disc would cost almost £30. Not cheap.

This would make a Photo CD player quite an expensive luxury and, quite apart from the cost, there's the nagging question of whether anyone would particularly want to watch their photos on the TV. For CD-ROM owners, however, the Photo CD idea is altogether more interesting, simply because it is a system for scanning in your own photographs and storing them as computer picture files.

Which means you can pop down to Boots with an armful of your favourite photographs, get the Photo CD disc back a week later, then transfer a picture to the hard drive of your PC as a PCX file, or to your Macintosh as a PICT file – the same Photo CD disc will work in either type of computer. And you can then use that picture in, say, a desktop publishing (DTP) package, maybe to illustrate a newsletter you produce for a club or society, or perhaps to make a poster for a

Kodak's Photo CD Player looks like a video recorder and can play audio CDs as well as show slideshows of your own photographs on the telly. As £200, half the price it originally cost, it's not actually bad value for gadget fiends.

school play, or even to create a very individual birthday card for someone.

A scanner that enables you to use photographs in a similar way – in full colour, from photographic negatives or transparencies – would cost around £1,000 for a basic model, and even then it takes a lot of practice to reproduce images with good clarity and depth of colour. So Photo CD is a cheap way for CD-ROM users to get their own photos scanned and delivered.

How you use Photo CD

The technology that makes Photo CD work is a variant on the CD-ROM X/A standard, so any CD-ROM drive of that type will be able to read Photo CD discs. Most adverts for CD-ROM drives say whether they will do Photo CD or not, and you might as well buy one that does, since it costs you no extra.

One of the advantages of Photo CD is that you can take a disc you already have back to Boots and get some extra pictures put on it. This means the disc will have data written to it in more than one 'session', so you also need a CD-ROM drive that has 'multi-session' capability. Again, this applies to most, but do check.

You can get your pictures transferred to Photo CD at either Boots or Kodak's own chain of photo processing shops – there's a branch of both in all decent-sized towns. Boots also have a colour leaflet about their Photo CD services.

First you have to sort out all the pictures you want done – negatives or transparencies can be used, or a mixture of both, but not prints. Slides are simple, but with negatives you will have to sort them out carefully. It's not too tricky if you just want a whole film done, or even if you want a whole strip of negs done, but if you have individual images from several different films, the photo shop will have to sort them in different envelopes, so as not to mix up the numbers. And if you only want one frame from a film, they will want just the strip with that frame on, not all the rest of the negatives from the film. Sorting out your neg strips carefully in advance will save a lot of time.

Exact prices vary according to where you go. There may be a set rate for the first 20 or 36 images, then you pay for each one above that; while Kodak shops charge more for single images from a strip of negatives than they do for the whole strip.

You will also have to pay extra if you want the pictures to appear in a specified order on the final disc (it all makes extra work for them). And if there is a chance that not all the pictures will fit on one disc (the limit is about 100 pictures per disc) then you will be asked whether you are willing to pay for a second disc for the over-run.

Then you will have to wait a week while the whole lot goes to Kodak's Ilford laboratories to be processed, so if you take them in on a Tuesday you will be picking up your disc the following Wednesday. Pay your money – 84 images cost us £48.95 – and take it home to try it.

Using Kodak Photo CD images on your computer

Before you can use a Photo CD disc in your CD-ROM drive you'll need the correct drivers, but they generally come free with the CD-ROM drives. On the Mac, you require a combination of the QuickTime extension and the Apple PhotoCD Access extension, both of which will normally be installed in your System folder by the install procedure of a new CD-ROM drive. On the PC you'll need the Photo Access software, which again will usually be supplied along with your CD-ROM driver software, but can be purchased separately for about £30.

What you then find on your Photo CD disc is five scanned computer images per picture, which vary greatly in file size. The smallest of the five is of very poor quality, scanned at a very low resolution, and is intended only for use as a postage stamp-sized 'thumbnail' image on what the software refers to as a "contact sheet", which will make immediate sense to photographers.

The remaining four scans are at varying degrees of resolution that are designed to suit the proper Kodak Photo CD players that display images on a TV screen. The second size is for quarter-screen preview images, the third is for full-screen, the fourth is for zoom enlargements and the fifth is an extra one which will mean that Photo CD can supply higher-resolution pictures when HDTV (high-definition television) starts coming into use. The great advantage of these five different sizes for computer use is that it gives you a choice of different resolutions so that you can pick an appropriate one for more or less any job you want to do. We'll go on to show how they can be used in a moment.

The Kodak Photo CD Player

When Kodak Photo CD was first launched, the price of the in-the-living-room 'black box' Photo CD player was rather steep, coming in at £299 for the basic PCD 265, or £369 for the PCD 865 which has added extras, most interestingly a 'zoom' enlargement feature.

These prices have now been substantially reduced to £149 and £199 respectively. When you consider that these devices are also high-quality bitstream audio CD players, the new prices make them pretty attractive. If you were on the point of buying a CD player anyway, the

Apple's PowerCD is not only a CD-ROM drive, but also an audio CD player, and a Photo CD player that can be plugged straight into your TV and used for Photo CD slideshows.

amount of extra technology you get by buying a Photo CD player instead works out to be very good value.

We tried out a PCD 865, and the pictures look excellent on a TV screen, sharp with bright colours. Many pictures which don't look too great as originals look an awful lot better on the screen. As an entertainment for family or friends, this new variant on the old-fashioned slideshow is excellent, and without all the fuss that used to make slideshows a bore. We'd recommend that if you do buy a PCD machine, you might as well pay the extra for the version with the zoom feature, because it really does add a lot of enjoyment.

Transferring Photo CD images to the computer

On the Mac you can just drag the image you want onto your Mac hard drive. On the PC you load it into the software from the CD, then save it out to your hard drive. It can be helpful to have a graphics package that loads images in Photo CD format, and on the PC, the latest version of the shareware image processing package *Paint Shop Pro* has this ability. Mac owners might be pleased to learn that there is a plug-in for Adobe *Photoshop* that enables it to load Photo CD images directly. What you'll probably end up with is a PICT graphics file on the Mac, or a PCX or TIFF file on the PC.

There is one small snag, however; the images are stored in a 'compressed' file format, and when you transfer them they become much larger. You also need a lot of RAM memory to manipulate the bigger sizes.

One slight problem we came across with the largest ones, suitable for professional use at full-page size, is that some machines simply can't handle the process of getting them to the hard drive. We found it was a bit hit-and-miss – some would transfer to our Macs OK, some wouldn't. But then you won't necessarily need to use the top-size ones, as we'll go on to explain.

One other important consideration is that the compression systems used to squeeze images on to the Photo CD do actually have a detrimental effect on the quality of the image. To get the best results, you will very often need to use an image processing program to sharpen the image, and to alter the brightness and contrast.

Using Photo CD images in DTP

Even though Photo CD seems quite expensive, at around 60p for each image it works out massively cheaper than professional scanning. And even if you have simpler needs than full-colour glossy magazines, it could still be a cheap way of getting decent pictures.

As we've said, there are five different graphics files for each of your Photo CD images. Each is of a different resolution, which is measured by the number of pixels across and down the image. The greater the number of pixels in the image, the higher the resolution and the more hard disk space the graphics file will take up.

To get the correct print quality, it's important to make sure you use an image of high enough resolution, but to avoid problems, you want to keep your image as small as possible. The best way to do this is first lay out your design in your DTP program. You then know what size your picture needs to be. Next, you have to work out what resolution your printing method uses, which will depend on whether you're planning to do it in black-and-white on a laser printer, in colour on a colour printer, or take it to your local bureau to be output.

For domestic output, with a print resolution measured in dots per inch (dpi), you will only need a fairly low-resolution image. Trial and error should help you work out at what size the pixels in the image effectively disappear. For professional-quality output, where much higher resolutions are measured in lines per inch (lpi), you'll need to choose a much higher resolution image. Here, Kodak have helped by providing a simple formula which will help you work out the correct resolution of image to use for different sizes and resolutions of print.

Take the figures for the desired size of the picture when printed (in inches), and the resolution of your output (in lpi) and you can use this simple formula to calculate the resolution, in pixels, you need.

Finally, before you actually print your correctly-sized image, further image processing might be a good idea. As well as adjusting the brightness and contrast of the image, and possibly sharpening it as well, an image processing package can be useful for other purposes. You should 'crop' the picture before using it in the DTP layout, cutting it down to the right shape, which also makes the graphics file smaller. You may also need to resize your image to the resolution your calculations tell you that you want.

You can also convert images to a lower number of colours – Photo CD pictures are full photo-quality 24-bit – which again cuts down the size of the graphics file. Alternatively, you could convert to shades of grey if you're printing in monochrome. There's one last thing it may be useful to do with your image processing software if you are planning to print in black-and-white, and that's add a half-tone screen. This breaks up the picture into little dots, like a newspaper photo, which can prevent it from blurring into a mess when printed on some output devices.

Graphics file sizes of Photo CD pictures

There are five different resolutions of graphics file for each Photo CD picture. The larger ones need lots of RAM memory. Here are Kodak's estimates of how much memory you need to load and edit the different sizes of image. You can, of course, use 'virtual memory' which is hard disk space that the program 'pretends' is RAM.

Resolution (in pixels)	Memory (in Mb)
128 x 192	2.5
256 x 384	3
512 x 768	7.5
1024 x 1536	15
2048 x 3072	30

How to choose the correct image resolution

First, lay out your document so that you know what actual, physical size you want your picture to be. Second, decide your output resolution. If your document is being professionally printed, they will suggest a resolution, very likely to be 150 or 300 lpi (lines per inch). You can use an output resolution that is equivalent to this figure, or a sensible fraction of it; so for 300 lpi output, 300 lpi, 150 lpi, 100 lpi or 75 lpi would all work. Then use this formula to calculate the pixel resolution of the image you want. We've printed the formula three ways round for the different calculations you may want to do.

If you want to work in centimetre sizes, you can convert lines per inch to lines per centimetre by dividing by 2.54.

number of pixels (width or height)
divided by
desired size (inches)
equals
resolution (lines per inch)

resolution (lines per inch)
multiplied by
desired size (inches)
equals
number of pixels (width or height)

number of pixels (width or height)
divided by
resolution (lines per inch)
equals
desired size (inches)

Kodak Photo Edge

WHAT DOES IT MEAN?

This is an image processing package designed for use with Photo CD images and available for both the Mac and PC. It's pretty basic, but that makes it simple to use and it does most of the things you need.

You can alter brightness, contrast or colour balance, you can mirror or rotate your picture, and you can sharpen or smooth the image. The package is very good for cropping and resizing pictures to the resolution you want. A handy tool even measures the number of pixels between any two points, which is great for judging cropped sizes.

You can convert a picture to 256 colours or to mono, you can save out in different file formats and you can add a variety of halftone screens if you want to print in black-and-white. Oh, and the manual is excellent.

What it lacks is a painting tool of some kind: if your picture has a hair or scratch showing, and sometimes they do, then you need to be able to pick up colours from the surrounding area of the picture and paint over the cracks. You can't. And it's too expensive for the average home user. If Kodak added a paint tool and charged £50 or £60, it could be very popular.

Kodak Shoebox

WHAT DOES IT MEAN?

This is a database for cataloguing Photo CD images, and the strange name is explained by the fact that Kodak's research told them that most people keep their photos in a shoebox.

But this program is far too powerful for the home user, and I'm sure professional photographers don't keep their pictures in shoeboxes. For pros who are going over to Photo CD – and many are – it would probably make a lot of sense. Other businesses that need to keep track of large numbers of pictures, such as publishers and photo libraries, would find it a boon, too.

What it does well, though this takes a lot of time to do, is enable you to set up lots of different description tags for images. So you might set up a database of landscapes and then be able to search for all the pictures of Scottish mountains taken in the morning light, in sunny weather, with walkers in. That sort of thing. Of course, you have to type in all the category information for each image, so setting up a good-sized database takes a lot of work.

At the price and given the investment in time it requires, this is one only for fairly committed businesses. It's not perfect – I find the 'read me' file of bugs alarming – but it will probably become an industry-wide standard, especially since its search system mirrors the Picture Exchange system which on-line photo libraries will be using.

Pro Photo CD

There is also a professional version of Photo CD, which has two main differences from the consumer version. One, you can get images on larger formats than 35mm transferred, up to 4-by-5-inch. Two, there is an extra scan of each image, at an even higher resolution of 4096 by 6144 pixels (that's a printed image of 20.7 inches by 40.96 inches at a 150 lpi resolution).

There's also a third difference, which is that you can only fit 25 five-by-fours on one disc, and a fourth difference, which is that you can't get it done at Boots. This is a bureau service. It costs a fair bit more than the domestic Photo CD, being closer to traditional repro scan prices, and is available from many repro companies, such as Laserbureau in London.

Chapter 14
Troubleshooting!

- Most-asked questions
- Hardware/software problems
- ...and much, much more!

Introduction

The beauty of CD-ROM is that it's generally very easy to set up and use a CD-ROM drive. But there are certain things people do get stuck on, so here's a quick review of some of the most frequently asked questions, and solutions to some of the most common problems. All of these are genuine enquiries which have been received by CD-ROM Today magazine.

Caddy or not?

Which is better, a CD-ROM drive that uses caddies, or one that doesn't?

It depends on your circumstances. There is no actual difference in how effectively they work, so you don't need to worry about that. A tray-style system, used by most PC drives, is more convenient if you swop discs a lot. A caddy will protect discs, and so is better for school, library or work situations, but caddies are expensive at about £5 each.

CD-R and optical drives

Are recordable CD-ROM machines the same as optical storage?

No, they're completely different. Optical (and, indeed, the so-called 'floptical') storage systems are removable-media storage that function exactly the same way as magnetic removable media, such as SyQuest drives. Expensive cartridges are used, and data can be written and re-written. Optical drives actually use a system similar to Sony's MiniDisc digital audio recording. Recordable CD-ROM, by contrast, writes data to a CD-ROM-style disc, and that data cannot then be changed or re-written.

Corrupted files (PC)

I was installing some CD-ROM software to the hard drive and the set-up failed half-way through. When I rebooted the PC, there were loads of new subdirectories full of files with names that were gibberish. Why?

Probably the File Allocation Table (FAT) which records where every files on your hard drive is stored has become corrupted, which can happen occasionally. It's a good idea to check for problems in the FAT, especially before using new software, using ScanDisk (MS-DOS 6.2) or ChkDsk (older versions of MS-DOS). These utilities will find problems before they get out of hand.

TOP TIP

It's always a good idea to make sure that you have sufficient hard disk space before you start an installation routine, because if the installer runs out of space and gives up before the end, it can leave a mess of files behind which are not properly allocated.

Disc won't eject (Mac)

My Mac's on a network, and quite often when I try to eject a disc it won't let me because it says other people are using it. What's going on?

There's a bug in the System which, when you are using File Sharing, often prevents you from ejecting a disc because it says the disc is in use on the network, even when it isn't. The only thing you can do is switch off File Sharing.

DoubleSpace problems?

I have read that CD-ROM discs may not run if I use DoubleSpace in MS-DOS 6.2 to increase my hard disk capacity. Is this true?

There shouldn't be any problems with 99% of CD-ROM software, but there always seems to be the odd game that refuses to run. In any case, though, the experts aren't generally in favour of using disk-doubling compression utilities – if you decide to stop using it you may find it tricky to sort out all the files you want to keep, and because of copyright problems Microsoft have now removed DoubleSpace from DOS.

Double-speed and single-speed

I notice that many CD-ROMs also have normal CD audio tracks on which can actually be played on an audio CD player, so does this mean they won't work on a double-speed drive?

No, because double-speed drives are actually dual-speed and so can run at either single or double speed – they sense whether a disc contains computer or audio data and play the disc at the appropriate speed. When you run a disc that has CD audio on, the drive will read the CD-ROM's header track and play at single-speed, and the animation in a disc like TuneLand, which uses a lot of CD audio, is all set up to run at the lower speed. Some discs use compressed, interleaved computer audio instead of CD-DA audio so that they can run at double-speed.

TOP TIP

To play discs with proper CD-DA audio, you need to check that the audio lead is connected properly from the CD-ROM drive to the sound card. Check this by playing an audio CD on your system and seeing whether the sound comes out of the speakers.

Drive make confusion (PC)

What's the difference between a Panasonic 562 and 563, or, for that matter, a Matsushita CD-ROM drive?

Matsushita is the parent company of Panasonic and uses that brand name in some countries, so there's no difference there. The 563 is the standard Panasonic drive, while the 562 is a slightly different version created for Creative Labs, the makers of Sound Blaster sound cards. However, either model can use a Sound Blaster Pro or a Sound Blaster 16 sound card as its interface, the difference being only the driver software – the 562 uses Creative's SBCD.SYS driver, while the 563 uses Panasonic's CDMKDE.SYS driver software. The only mechanical difference between the two models is that the 563 has a built-in self-cleaning assembly.

Drive not reading (Mac)

I've just switched on my CD-ROM drive, but when I put a disc in it it doesn't appear on the screen. What's wrong?

TOP TIP

If you've switched the CD-ROM drive on while the Mac is already switched on, the Mac may not recognise it. Use a SCSI installer like SCSI Probe to tell the Mac the drive is now running, or simply restart the Mac.

Drive not working (PC)

I've just fitted a CD-ROM drive inside my PC and it's not working at all. What could I have done wrong?

The best thing to do if you've installed the hardware yourself is to remove it all and repeat the whole process, just to make sure you've done it properly. Otherwise, check the following.

Software

- Look for a typing error in any of your PC's set-up files that you have modified (autoexec.bat and config.sys).
- Check that you have altered the LASTDRIVE command in config.sys appropriately, and ensure that it's placed before the device driver statement. Make sure you have consistently used the right device name, not one that's already in use, throughout all the files (generally D: for a new CD-ROM drive, or E: for a second drive).
- Make sure you have the correct device driver installed for your CD-ROM drive Refer to the manual to check the driver filename.
- Check that you haven't enabled expanded memory when you don't need it.
- Check that all the settings in the config.sys file are exactly the same as those in the autoexec.bat file.

Interface (controller) card or sound card settings

- Check that the interrupt (IRQ) settings are as they should be, and not interfering with any other device. These are often set using 'jumpers', and your manual will help you get them right.
- Check that the 'base port' or 'I/O address' settings – areas of memory set aside for the hardware device – are not in conflict with any other hardware.

Hardware

- Check that cables are installed the right way round, and that no pins on connectors are bent or missing.

- **Check that the power supply has the capacity to run all the hardware you have attached to it. You may need to install an uprated power supply.**
- **If you have a SCSI drive, make sure the terminator plug is fitted properly and that the SCSI ID number is unique.**
- **If all else fails, remove the cables (power and data) and replace them with new ones, just in case there's a break in one of the cables.**

Drive speeds

My CD-ROM drive is supposedly a high-performance model with a seek time of 350ms, but the manual says that this is the '1/3 stroke' seek time, and that the 'full seek time' is a much slower 650ms. Have I been ripped off?

Seek times measure how quickly the read head can jump around the disc to find a new bit of data. On average, the head will only need to jump a third of the way across the disc, so the '1/3 stroke' seek time is the standard measurement of how fast a drive can find data. No, they're not pulling the wool over your eyes.

EMS memory change to set-up files won't work (PC)

I was a little tentative about changing my autoexec.bat and config.sys files to use EMS for playing DOS games, but I took the plunge in the end and edited the files. When I reset my PC using the CTRL-ALT-DEL key combination, however, the changes did not take effect and the games would still not run. Why?

The problem is that a 'soft' reboot leaves the RAM chips powered and so will not necessarily clear the memory of the original

configurations, so when the PC restarts, it's still using the original set-up. The answer is to perform a 'hard' reboot, by switching your PC off for about 30 seconds, then switching on again.

TOP TIP

Always remember to make back-up copies of the start-up files before editing them, and also remember that the best option can be to have a start-up that offers you choices of configuration, as described elsewhere in this book.

Gold discs won't play on Panasonic drive (PC)

I've been using a JVC ROM-Maker to produce gold CD-ROM masters, but when I try to play them on a PC equipped with a Panasonic drive, they sometimes won't work. Why?

There's a problem with the way the combination of a Sound Blaster sound card and a Panasonic drive handles multi-session (Orange Book standard) discs. If your disc has less that 580Mb of data you won't notice a problem. If you are using the longer, 640Mb (74 minutes) discs and storing more then 580Mb, the drive will imagine that all the data over 580Mb is in a separate session. Creative Labs are releasing a new version of the driver software which cures the problem.

Hard disk drives (speed of)

I'm told that hard drives are a lot faster at reading data than CD-ROM drives, so is it beneficial for the two to work together, and is this how CD games that save your progress work?

Basically, yes. Most applications transfer an icon and a main control program to your hard drive. Programs like encyclopedias will often store large data files on your hard drive so that they can search for

articles much more quickly. Games save scores to the hard drive, but most other CD applications also save set-up data and preferences.

Hard disk sizes

I am thinking about getting a CD-ROM drive and upgrading my system, which has an 80Mb hard drive and 4Mb of RAM. Conventional wisdom is that I need a hard drive of at least 100Mb – is this true? What about for music and Photo CD applications?

Most CD ROM software installs a fairly small program file on your hard drive and some software puts a slightly larger data file on too. So long as you don't use dozens of different CD-ROM discs, or provided you are willing to delete these files from your hard drive and re-install them only when you need them, you won't run out of hard disk space just for running CD-ROM discs.

Photo CD images, however, will take up large amounts of hard disk space and need large amounts of RAM. Music sequencing is fine, especially if you're using the built-in instruments in a PC sound card, which are often like mini-synthesisers, but if you want to sample sounds, again a large amount of disk space and RAM would be needed. This is why the MPC2 standard calls for 160Mb hard drives, and why we recommend at least 8Mb of RAM for graphics or music.

Install problems with single-speed drives (PC)

I have a single-speed CD-ROM in my 66MHz 486DX2 PC. When installing programs from a CD under Windows, it often stops with a disc error and the Retry or Ignore buttons come up. It will always install the program eventually, but I often have to click Retry several times. Why?

Simply enough, the single-speed drive can't supply data fast enough and the install program gets fed up waiting and asks what's going on. Making sure the CD is clean might help, but the only real answer is a faster CD-ROM drive.

IRQ settings (PC)

When I go to install CD-ROM software, some discs suggest the default Sound Blaster IRQ setting is 7, while others say it's IRQ 5. Which is right, and what difference does it make?

When you fit additional expansion cards to a PC, each one must have a different Interrupt ReQuest (IRQ) number so that the PC can tell them apart. If more than one card uses the same IRQ setting, the PC will often get mixed up and crash. But not always. Older Sound Blaster cards used an IRQ setting of 7, but this same IRQ number is used by the printer port (LPT1) and it transpired that people with Sound Blasters fitted would get a horrible screeching noise out of the speakers when printing, because the PC sent all the print data to the sound card as well as to the printer. That's why newer Sound Blaster cards generally use IRQ 5. With any card, you can change the jumper settings on the board to change the IRQ it uses. Check the manual for how to do so. Other important settings are the memory address (usually 220H), and the DMA channel, which will usually be channel 5 for 16-bit cards And channel 1 for 8-bit cards.

Joysticks won't work (PC)

I've got a game that can use two joysticks and my PC has two joystick ports, but neither of them works properly. What can I do?

Many PCs have a joystick port built in to the disk controller attached to the motherboard, and many sound cards add another one.

However, the two will conflict with each other. The only way to get one of them working is to disconnect the other one, and the only way to get two joysticks working is to disconnect both and add a special dedicated games controller with two joystick ports, which will only cost about £25. Make sure the games controller you buy can handle the same speed as your PC's processor, e.g. 33MHz.

Memory shortage in Windows

I used to have a problem with Microsoft Art Gallery crashing when I tried to access the help system. I've re-installed it, but now I often get the message 'insufficient memory', and it won't run. The same thing also happens with some other software, and I've tried using MEMMAKER, but to no avail. I have 4Mb of RAM. What's up?

Your 4Mb should be plenty. It is said that there is a bug in Windows 3.0 and 3.1 that makes it think it's run out of memory even when it hasn't. If you quit all other applications before running a new one, you should be OK. Also, try using a permanent Windows swop file, which will make sure Windows has enough disk space.

TOP TIP

When a Windows application crashes, try using the key combination of Ctrl-Alt-Del, which should help you quit the crashed program and return to Windows. Failing that, use the same combination again to perform a soft reboot. Try not to reset the computer by switching it off unless you can't make it respond to anything else, and refer to the advice under 'Temp files on the PC' elsewhere in this chapter.

Memory shortage on the Mac

Sometimes a program that used to open perfectly well fails to open, and I get a message telling me that I haven't got enough memory. What can I do to stop this happening?

Mac programs need a single, continuous chunk of RAM to load into. Some programs, when you quit out of them, fail to free up RAM properly, while some badly-written software, particularly Extensions, will stay sitting in the middle of an area of memory so that the free areas on either side are not big enough. The immediate solution is to restart the Mac, freeing up all RAM. A long-term solution is to try to find out which program is messing up your memory, and stop using it.

You will also notice that the Clipboard stores data in RAM and is only cleared when you restart, so if you have copied or cut a large item like a picture, it may still be sitting there eating up your RAM. You could restart, but the easiest thing is to replace the large item on the Clipboard with a tiny item, perhaps by selecting one letter in a file name and copying it.

Monitor too small

I've bought a 15-inch monitor but it looks a little small, and when I measured the diagonal across the visible screen it turned out to be only just over 14 inches. Have I been ripped off?

Monitor makers are only obliged to quote the actual size of the tube, not how much of it is visible when the tube is placed inside the case, so for many monitors, the visible area is much smaller than the actual quoted size. Sometimes, a 15-inch monitor might have only 13.5 inches visible, so you're not doing badly.

The same will apply to a smaller monitor, so a '14-inch' monitor will have a visible screen smaller than 14 inches, so you're still ahead of the game.

The other advantage of 15-inch monitors is that they usually have an FST (flatter, squarer tube) so you can use the height and width controls to fill the screen right to the edges, and the lack of

curvature means you get a great display, ideal for using Windows in 800 by 600 mode.

PowerMac running Windows CD-ROMs

If I get a PowerMac and run SoftWindows, can I use Windows CD-ROM titles in the internal CD-ROM drive, and are there any problems?

SoftWindows can run Windows CDs directly, but you need 16Mb of RAM to run it properly and even then it will only emulate Windows in standard mode rather than 386 Enhanced mode. This means that anything that uses virtual memory won't work, and any discs that check the Windows mode also won't work. Sadly, that means most decent titles won't run on a PowerMac with SoftWindows.

RealMagic affecting screen displays

My ReelMagic board seems to mess up all the colours in DOS games. Surely I don't have to disconnect the card each time I want to do something that doesn't use MPEG video?

The ReelMagic is impressive, but it often seems to be very difficult to set up and use, mainly because it tries to work beyond the capabilities of the features connector on the video card it connects to. Anyway, one simple way to bypass the card is to disconnect the monitor, remove the dummy connector from the output socket on your video card, and connect your monitor back up directly to the video card when you're not using the RealMagic.

Sound not working on video clips

When I run video clips there are often problems with the sound. Sometimes it's distorted, and sometimes it jumps, skipping bits of sound. What's wrong?

Distortion on sound clips can be due to the original recording being rather dodgy, but is often also due to the use of extreme levels of compression. Some sound files will have hisses and buzzes which have been created as a side effect of the compression used. The problem of skipping bits of sound is a common one and, unfortunately, cannot really be solved. It's because the video is running at a frame rate which is higher than your hardware can easily transfer.

Speaker interference

I've bought a pair of powered speakers that are magnetically shielded to stop them from interfering with the monitor, but one of them still makes the display go wobbly. Why is this?

The shielding prevents the magnets in the speaker from messing up the screen display, but probably one of your speakers contains a power supply transformer which converts AC mains current to DC electricity to power the amplifier. Check by switching off and seeing if the wobbling stops. The only solution is to move the powered one further away, but you can buy speakers where the power transformer is in a block that's incorporated into the mains plug, a good long way away from the actual speakers, which prevents this problem occurring.

Speeding up with a cache (PC)

I have a triple-speed CD-ROM drive and I'm using *Norton SpeedCache* to help speed it up, but still some software seems very slow. Is there anything I can do, perhaps with another cache utility?

Unfortunately CD-ROM drives are much slower than the hard disk drives which we're all used to, and there's not a lot you can do about it. Caching utilities won't really make a noticeable difference. Your best bet is to hope for better-programmed applications that are careful about where on the CD they store data, and make good use of data files installed to the hard drive.

Swop files in Windows

I read that it is better to use a permanent Swop File in Windows rather than a temporary one, so I used the Virtual Memory screen in the 386 Enhanced section of Control Panels to set this up, but when I returned to DOS I found that I had somehow lost 20Mb of hard disk space. Is it worth it, and what is a swop file anyway?

When RAM runs short, as it does when you are running several programs even if you have quite large amounts, Windows uses hard disk space as a temporary storage area for the data it's supposed to be playing with in RAM. The technique is known as 'virtual memory', because the hard disk is pretending to be RAM, and the area of the hard disk that Windows uses as RAM is called a swop file. If you have Windows set up to use a temporary swop file, it will have to spend time looking for the necessary hard disk space each time Windows starts up, which slows it down, and it will tend to use any available fragments of hard disk space, thus scattering the swop file around the hard drive and further slowing things down.

When you set up a permanent swop file, Windows marks out in advance the area of hard disk space that it will use as virtual

memory, and won't let anything else use that space. For that reason you will lose the use of that area of your hard disk – hence the 20Mb drop in available memory – but Windows will load quicker, and the swop file will always be a contiguous chunk of hard disk space, so speeding up its operation.

Temp files on the PC

In my DOS sub-directory I have found a whole bunch of files with a .TMP extension. I'm wondering where they came from, and whether it's safe to delete them.

Temporary files, with a .TMP extension, are often created by Windows. They are used to store data when Windows has run out of RAM to work in. Normally, Windows will delete the temporary files after it has finished using them, but if your PC crashes before it gets the chance to delete the temporary files the deletion process will not be carried out and you end up with lots of unnecessary files cluttering up the hard drive. It is perfectly safe to get rid of them, but do not delete .TMP files while Windows is running, because you might delete one that Windows is still using, and so Windows will crash.

TOP TIP

There's a handy way to organise where .TMP files are stored on your hard drive. Add the line SET TEMP=C:\TEMP to your autoexec.bat file, and then create a directory called TEMP on your hard drive, and you will find that all .TMP files are stored in that directory, making them easier to find and tidy up.

Video CD: same in US and UK?

I'm going to the States soon and I'm thinking about buying an MPEG card like the RealMagic to play Video CD discs. Will an American card work with my British PC?

American TV and video tapes use the NTSC system, which is not compatible with European PAL video and TV. With Video CD, however, the MPEG format is the same all over the world, so you can use a card bought anywhere and play discs from anywhere in the world.

Video for both PC and Mac?

I always thought AVI (Video for Windows) files were video clips for Windows PCs, and QuickTime was video for the Mac, but recently I bought a Windows disc that had a QT extension on it. Does this mean QuickTime works on Windows?

Yes. It is possible to get run-time versions of QuickTime for the PC and even run-time AVI players for the Mac, which convert the video clips to an appropriate format on the fly as the video is played. This is ideal for developers who have created their software on one platform, but want it to work on the other. A good example is the game Myst, which was created on the Mac and so uses QuickTime videos on both Mac and PC.

Video for Windows error

When running Video for Windows clips, I often receive an error message that reads 'APPLICATION ERROR MMTASK CAUSED A GENERAL PROTECTION FAULT IN MODULE 256-1280.DRV AT 0007:0B44'. What an this mean?

You've probably already discovered that Windows error messages are almost always completely unintelligible. This one means you're having problems with the graphics display – the software that's expired is for running Windows in 256-colour mode with a high-resolution display. Try setting up your screen driver in advance to run in 256 colours at 640-by-480 or 800-by-600 resolution. Alternatively, contact the supplier of your system or your video card to see if there is any updated driver software available that cures the problem.

Unfortunately, the problem of graphics cards running most Windows software, but crashing with particular examples, is quite a widespread one: the card is usually not at fault, and you will find that updated driver software is available and will cure the problem.

Index

Other titles from Future Publishing

Copies of the following books are available direct from Future Publishing Limited, Freepost (BS4900) Somerton, Somerset, TA11 6BR. Alternatively they are available in all good bookshops. Retailers can order copies from our distributors, Computer Bookshops, on 021 706 1250

All you need to know imprint

The overall aim of the imprint is to cover the software features most users use most of the time, enabling the reader to get up and running as quickly as possible.

The books assume a familiarity with the Windows environment, and all are written with a series of helpful icons highlighting important information. They are written with a walk-through tutorial style, and make extensive use of illustrations and screen grabs.
All books will be suitable for Beginners and Intermediate users

All you need to know about PCs

by Geoff Oakshott
ISBN 1-85870-055-8
Size 220mm(H) x 150mm(W)
Pages 350
Price £14.95
Publication Date November 1994
Order no: FBB0558

The first book of the 'All you need to know' imprint, serves as an introduction to PCs and also includes 'hints and tips' suitable for the more experienced user. Includes an introduction to computing – the hardware and software, windows and DOS operating systems. If you haven't bought your PC yet this book tells you what you're in for. If you have it'll make it work for you.

All you Need to Know about WordPerfect for Windows (v 6.0 & 6.1)

by Stephen Copestake
ISBN 1-85870-056-6
Size 220mm(H) x 150mm(W)
Pages 320
Price £12.95
Publication Date November 1994
Order no: FBB0566

Covers version 6.0 with the added refinements included in the latest release 6.1. As well as providing a complete insight into WordPerfect for Windows, the book provides a quick check list of all the new features for those upgrading from previous versions.

All you need to know about Excel 5.0 for Windows

by Stephen Copestake
ISBN 1-85870-057-4
Size 220mm(H) x 150mm(W)
Pages 320
Price £12.95
Publication Date November 1994
Order no: FBB0574

This book takes a jargon free look at Excel 5.0 for Windows - it covers the features which most users use, most of the time. Icons draw your attention to useful hints, tips and key techniques, while the tutorial style and liberal use of illiustrations lets you gain a thorough understanding of the software in the shortest possible time.

All you Need to Know about Lotus 1-2-3 (v 4.0 & 5.0) for Windows

by Ian Sinclair
ISBN 1-85870-058-2
Size 220mm(H) x 150mm(W)
Pages 300
Price £12.95
Publication Date November 1994
Order no: FBB 0582

The book covers all the main elements of this leading spreadsheet package including its often unexploited data handling capabilities. In order to keep you up to date with all the latest developments the book includes all the refinements of the latest release, version 5.0.

All you Need to Know about the INTERNET

by Davey Winder
ISBN 1-85870-064-7
Size 230mm(H) x 185mm(W)
Pages 350
Price £14.95
Publication Date November 1994
Order no: FBB0647

A comprehensive guide to exploring the network written by the UK's leading communications expert Davey Winder. Whether you are a beginner or one of the original netsurfers this book will unlock the 'information super-highway'.

Money Management imprint

Money Management with Quicken 6.0 for DOS

by Jean Miles
ISBN 1-85870-012-4
Size 205mm x 120mm
Pages 230
Price £8.95
Publication Date May 1994
Order no: FBB0124

Now into its third print run the book has enjoyed success exceeded only by the software sales!! and is every bit a best seller. It serves as a comprehensive guide to all the facilities of Intuit's DOS version of this leading finance package.

Money Management with Quicken 3.0 for Windows

by Jean Miles
ISBN 1-85870-017-5
Size 220mm x 150mm
Pages 280

Price £12.95
Publication Date April 1994
Order no: FBB0175

The second Quicken book from the pen of Jean Miles, this book has the Official backing of the software publishers, Intuit Software. A comprehensive look at this latest release of Quicken. This book is already established on the path to best seller status.

Money Management with Sage Moneywise 2.0 for Windows

by Jean Miles
ISBN 1-85870-043-4
Size 220mm x 150mm
Pages 250
Price £12.95
Publication Date October 1994
Order no: FBB0434

The third Money Management book from Jean Miles. Covers all the features of SageSoft's entry level package Moneywise. As with all the Money Management books it has the full endorsement of the software developers Sage.

Money Management with Microsoft Money 3.0 for Windows

by Andrew Marlow
ISBN 1-85870-044-2
Size 220mm x 150mm
Pages 280
Price £12.95
Publication Date October 1994
Order no: FB 0442

The fourth book of the imprint, written for Microsoft's latest version of their personal accounting package, Money 3.0.

Professional imprint

The Complete Desktop Publishing Guidebook

by Simon Williams & Geoffrey Oakshott
ISBN 1-85870-003-5
Size 235mm x 185mm
Pages 470
Price £24.95
Publication Date October 1994
Order no: FBB0035

A thorough insight into desktop publishing and design. This book provides all the advise and guidance on how to use dtp as an effective business tool. From the Publishers of PC Plus magazine.

Successful Business Accounting with Sage Sterling +2 Version 2

by Andrew Marlow
ISBN 1-85870-013-2
Size 235mm x 185mm
Pages 300
Price £24.95
Publication Date June 1994
Order no: FBB0132

A comprehensive look at the Sage +2 range of business products, comes complete with a free, complete copy of the Bank Interest Calculator software direct from Sage UK, with a number of business templates produced by the Author. Another officially endorsed books from Future Publishing.

The Complete Access Workbook

by Arthur Tennick
ISBN 1-85870-011-6
Size 223mm x 190mm
Pages 250

Price £17.95
Publication Date May 1994
Order no: FBB0116

A comprehensive database package requires something similar from a book. The Complete Access Workbook provides something for every type of user whether an absolute beginner or a professional programmer. It will guide you through the process of designing your database.

The Modem and Communications Guidebook

by Sue Schofield
ISBN 1-85870-000-0
Size 235mm x 185mm
Pages 350
Price £19.95
Publication Date November 1993
Order no: FBB0000

Written and researched in the UK, this book makes communications easy to learn, productive and trouble-free. Clear explanations of all the basic ideas without the unnecessary jargon, make the process of going on-line painless and straightforward. This book has very quickly established itself as a best seller. Book includes free comms software and CIX subscription.

Windows 3.1 HelpScreen

by Arthur Tennick
ISBN 1-85870-001-9
Size 223mm x 190mm
Pages 350
Price £19.95
Publication November 1993
Order no: FBB0019

Provides the straight forward answers to all the questions you might have about Windows - this book is for those with a basic familiarity with Windows but who wish to progress and quickly build their expertise. With a wealth of Windows books available it is reassuring to know you have the hallmark of authority from the UK's leading PC magazine PC Plus.

The PC Plus HelpScreen Collection

by Barry Thomas
ISBN 1-85870-002-7
Size 240mm x 205mm
Price £14.95 (includes disk)
Pages 150
Publication Date October 1993
Order no: FBB0027

A compilation of the last two years of HelpScreen pages within PC Plus. All material has been edited and rewritten to provide accessible time saving information.

The Software Guide

Size 240mm x170mm
Pages 450
Price £24.95
Publication Date March 1994
Order no: PSG003

The authoritative new directory of IBM-compatible PC software, this book comes to you from the publishers of the Britain's best selling PC magazine, PC Plus. It provides details of more than 3000 software products including hardware requirements, price and feature analysis.

Future Books Priority Order Form

You can use this tear-off coupon to order any of the Future Publishing books described on the previous pages. Simply fill in the details in the spaces provided and post this coupon (or a photocopy), together with payment, in an envelope to the following address:

Future Book Orders, Future Publishing Ltd, Freepost (BS4900), Somerton, Somerset TA11 6BR

Your name ....

Your address ....

.... Postcode ....

Your signature ....

Please send me (tick as appropriate):

	Title	Code	Price
☐	All you need to know about PCs	FBB0558	£14.95
☐	All you need to know about WordPerfect for Windows (versions 6.0 & 6.1)	FBB0566	£12.95
☐	All you need to know about Excel 5.0 for Windows	FBB0574	£12.95
☐	All you need to know about Lotus 1-2-3 (versions 4.0 & 5.0) for Windows	FBB0582	£12.95
☐	All you need to know about CD-ROM	FBB0590	£14.95
☐	All you need to know about the Internet	FBB0647	£14.95
☐	Money Management with Quicken 6.0 for DOS	FBB0124	£8.95
☐	Money Management with Quicken 3.0 for Windows	FBB0175	£12.95
☐	Money Management with Sage Moneywise 2.0 for Windows	FBB0434	£12.95
☐	Money Management with Microsoft Money 3.0 for Windows	FBB0442	£12.95
☐	The Complete Desktop Publishing Guidebook	FBB0035	£24.95
☐	Successful Business Accounting with Sage Sterling +2 Version 2	FBB0132	£24.95
☐	The Complete Access Workbook	FBB0116	£17.95
☐	The Modem and Communications Guidebook	FBB0000	£19.95
☐	Windows 3.1 Helpscreen	FBB0019	£19.95
☐	The PC Plus Helpscreen Collection	FBB0027	£14.95
☐	The Software Guide	PSG003	£24.95

Amount enclosed (Make cheques, P/Os etc. payable to Future Publishing Ltd.)

Method of payment (tick one): VISA ☐ ACCESS ☐ CHEQUE ☐ POSTAL ORDER ☐

CARD NUMBER ☐☐☐☐ ☐☐☐☐ ☐☐☐☐ ☐☐☐☐

EXPIRY DATE ☐☐ ☐☐

Tick here if you do not wish to receive direct mail from other companies ☐

Now send this coupon (or a photocopy) and your payment to the address on the front of this coupon.. You will not need a stamp when you post this order and postage and packing are free. There are no extra costs. Please allow 28 days for delivery.

AYNTKCD